D1073963

RODNEY LEGG

D-DAY DORSET

DORSET PUBLISHING COMPANY
WINCANTON PRESS NATIONAL SCHOOL NORTH STREET
WINCANTON SOMERSET BA9 9AT

For Barrie and Philip White

Publishing details. First published 1994. Copyright Rodney Legg © 1994. Published by Dorset Publishing Company at the Wincanton Press, National School, North Street, Wincanton, Somerset BA9 9AT (telephone 01963 32583).

Printing credits. Layout by Rodney Legg with typesetting input by Tim Wike in Bristol and output by Mediatec at 63 Santos Road, Wandsworth, London SW18 1NT (telephone 0181-870 6692). Photographic screenprints by Fred Bateman at FWB Printing, Bennett's Mead, Wincanton BA9 9EB. Printed in Wiltshire by John Langley at the Fairwood Press, Dilton Marsh, Westbury BA13 3SW (telephone 01373 822044).

Photographic coverage. All contemporary photographs provided either by private British or American sources or courtesy of the United States National Archives, Washington, District of Columbia.

Distribution. Orders in Dorset serviced by Maurice Hann from 36 Langdon Road, Parkstone, Poole, Dorset BH14 9EH (telephone 01202 738248). Other orders direct to the publisher at Wincanton Press, National School, North Street, Wincanton, Somerset BA9 9AT (telephone 01963 32583).

International standard book number ISBN 0 948699 42 6

C·O·N·T·E·N·T·S

6-7 June 1944. Emblem of the United States 1st Infantry Division (left), the 'Fighting Firsts' who will sail for Omaha Beach from Weymouth and Portland, on D-Day. They are to be reinforced on D-Day plus 1 by the 2nd United States Infantry Division, whose slogan is 'Second to None'. Their emblem is a shield with a five-pointed star that features an Indian head (right).

I·N·T·R·O·D·U·C·T·I·O·N

"You don't know how good North America looks till you see er a-slippin' over the horizon," said Master Sergeant Horn who arrived in the luxury liner *Mauretania*, cruising at a constant 25 knots with a change of course every seven minutes. The overcrowding and the hammocks made sure that the GIs did not travel in pre-war style.

Betty Mackay was a London evacuee who found herself at Burton Bradstock on the Dorset coast when it became a colossal armed camp. Travel was already restricted with "Military Control" passports that dated back to 1940. Betty would meet Sergeant Horn and his mates at the time when conflict was beginning to drag: "Life became stagnant and dreary after four years of war. Younger children like us had never known anything different. Rationing was not as tight as in the towns, because the countryside can always look after itself with extra goodies that the administrators cannot touch, but all the old luxuries had ceased to exist. So too had petrol."

Then, in December 1943, their world was transformed. The Yanks were coming: "Blooming big lorries and continuous lines of Sherman tanks knocked bits off our buildings and brought mountains of stores that were strewn across dozens of fields. Timber and Nissen hut encampments, each little building snug with its tortoise stove, mushroomed around the village."

Word spread, of course, as to what was to follow: "Midge we called the female version of Lord Haw-Haw who told us over the German wireless broadcasts that an amphibious landing would be at a tremendous cost in these young American lives. They too could have been under no illusions. They made Christmas 1943 the best any of us had ever had. For us it was gum, chocolates and sweets. Scotch whisky reappeared and it was everyone's first ever meal of turkey with cranberry sauce. They were so full of vitality and joy. Carols quickly turned into *Roll me over* and *Roll out the barrel*."

Overhead there was still the occasional German raider but rural England was now no longer defenceless. An Anti-Aircraft battalion parked on the hill above Abbotsbury to await its "Shooting Month" on Salisbury Plain. One evening Betty and friends heard a German bomber and saw the sky ripped open with searchlights: "There was more noise and fireworks than you've ever seen, and yet the plane went straight on through it and away the other side. It wasn't going to be quite as easy as they liked to think."

Black faces were a culture shock, particularly noticeable as they came in segregated units. The stone terraced houses of Portland's Reforne district witnessed a Wild West style gunfight as black and white troops took up their rifles and backed into doorways on opposite sides of the street. Shots were exchanged until two jeep loads of 'Snowballs' – the white-helmeted US Military Police – drew up and proceeded to baton charge, swiping the head of each offender in turn.

British bobby Bill Chapple had never seen anything like it, though he felt that by their instant contribution to road accident figures even an unarmed American Army would probably be able to sweep its way to Berlin by applied disregard of the highway code.

One of the bits of old England to take a knock that Christmas was the King's Arms inn at Longham, between Ringwood and Poole, where a heavy tank careered into the public bar. The side of the building would have collapsed but for the turret of the tank which ended up supporting the bedroom floor. "I was in bed there at the time," said Michael Weaver, the landlord's son, who was recovering from a bout of influenza. One soldier in the tank was slightly hurt but all the occupants of the bar, in the process of leaving at closing time, had remarkable escapes.

Halifax bombers, towing gliders night and day in the endless series of practice missions, lifted constantly from Tarrant Rushton. Pegasus was the emblem of the British 6th Airborne Division and became the name of the first bridge they took, which the French demolished on the eve of its fiftieth anniversary celebrations. Theirs was the highest invasion profile of all, and everyone knew we had hordes of airborne troops, though not that Barbara Cartland invented the idea of putting them in gliders.

There was a certain inevitable fall-out and for a while it seemed that Halifaxes were crashing all over Dorset.

Security tightened on the Dorset coast. "We had to call on every house and do an inventory on the occupants," remembered Portland policeman Bill Chapple. "That was a job. People were often rude, and who could blame them, with us poking our noses into their affairs. Each person in every household was checked and if they had no excuse for being in Portland they were given twenty-four hours to leave."

The inhabitants already knew of major accidents and calamities. "I saw Castletown Pier stacked high with bodies," said Cyril Brown of Portland. "We had twelve Americans lost in a tank landing craft on the Chesil Beach in the October after D-Day, but the big disaster was before. It happened off the same place, when German E-boats got among a convoy of American tank landing ships. Teams of Navy divers worked for days to recover the identity discs from the bodies still down there."

This was the night of 27 April 1944, before the big practice landings at Slapton Sands, Devon, and a total of 441 United States soldiers were killed or drowned, together with 197 seamen. The vessels were intercepted as they rounded Portland Bill. Coast defence guns remained silent because of the number of Americans who were in the water.

The operation to recover their body tags reassured Allied Naval Headquarters that none had been fished out alive from the sea by the Germans and taken prisoner. Confirmation of their demise was accompanied by immense feelings of relief. "This cloud's silver lining," as it was put in a secret memo, was the assurance that the invasion plans had not leaked to the enemy.

Sherborne's dead Americans of 30 March 1944 are the continuing victims of Winston Churchill's cautionary dictum: "The truth, in wartime, must be protected by a cloak of lies."

In 1989 they were given, belatedly, a plaque outside the Abbey, behind the town's war memorial. It lists twenty-nine names. Others, in accounts collected by Sherborne historian Gerald Pitman, have been insistent that the death-toll was as high as thirty-nine, forty or even 140.

That certainly extends to the precise cause of their deaths. All that is agreed is that it was an explosion. Most accounts then say that the truck ran over a live mine. It was either an anti-tank or anti-personnel weapon and the vehicle contained others which exploded at the same moment.

Hereon the documents diverge into two quite different explanations. Firstly, the mines were there because the United States Army was using live mines in a realistic exercise; this was only two months before D-Day and that would have been normal practice. Alternatively, claim papers from Washington which have been released following their freedom of information legislation, a string of mines has been smuggled into the area between Sherborne Castle and Haydon and planted there by German agents.

Confusing both accounts is the device of "moving events" which was practised by officialdom, the censors and the press from 1940 onwards. No one in the spring of 1944 was going to announce that a huge American army was gathering on the Dorset coast. The Germans knew the Americans were here but we were encouraging them to believe that the actual invasion would be from Sussex and Kent, across the narrower seas. Some of the American families were told the accident happened in Kent but others heard nothing until after 6 June when they were told the men had been killed in the D-Day landings.

In the case of the Sherborne explosion there was an additional reason for the deliberate disinformation being followed by longer term misinformation. I am now sure, as a result of correspondence and discussion with witnesses – all of whom were at a very safe distance – that I have established the precise location of the explosion and that this proves an answer for the tissue of lies.

It occurred at Ordnance Survey grid reference ST 650 159, which is 500 yards south-south-east of Sherborne Castle and in the field on the south side of Castleton public footpath number 6 which runs from The Slopes to Haydon Lodge.

The reason for "locational sensitivity" as it was called in an American letter is that this spot was within the confines of United States Army Hospital 228th Camp Unit, operating under the auspices of the International Red Cross in and around Haydon Park. Indeed they contravened the Geneva convention.

Because of that the Germans were blamed. The story was allowed to gather credence that two "enemy agents" – named as Kurt Henlein and Ernst Buchner – had infiltrated the camp and planted a string of mines on an army physical training course. The two agents would be executed by the British military at Salisbury in May 1944. How convenient – smuggling one landmine into a restricted area would seem possible, but the acquisition and placement of a lorry-load is less credible.

That there was a huge explosion cannot be doubted, if only by the fact that none of the members of the 294th Engineer Combat Battalion were injured. All in the vicinity, including those standing some distance away, were killed instantly.

"It was the loudest explosion I ever heard," said ex-Fosters schoolboy Tod Frost, who became a post-war Bristol policeman. "We were told by the Americans that they were practising mine laying when the lorry carrying the live mines rolled back over one which had just been placed in position."

He was working at the time for Arthur Jennings of Horsecastles Farm, which had expanded under the emergency agricultural arrangements to include 80 acres of Sherborne Park. Jennings and his workers, including

Frost who had just left school, were threshing a corn rick beside the private road in front of Sherborne Castle, on 30 March 1944

"At about midday there was a tremendous explosion. One of the vehicles disintegrated and several others were damaged. I was on the corn rick pitching sheaves on to the threshing machine and the Land Army girl who was bond cutting on the machine itself was hurled by the blast in a heap on top of me, a predicament I would have enjoyed under different circumstances. She was most fortunate not to have been impaled in a pitchfork."

The threshing machine – "a huge contraption" – lurched against the corn rick and then righted itself. "Had the rick been lower, the machine would have toppled over completely."

For a while the farm workers thought they might have been witnessing realistic war-games. It was a training field and inexplicable manoeuvres and explosions were not unknown, though not previously from that particular area.

"Our worst fears were confirmed, however," Tod Frost continued, "after the ambulances had returned to the camp. Open lorries passed along the road directly beneath us. We could see rows of mutilated bodies covered by their comrades, as best they could, with ground sheets. It was nevertheless an appalling sight."

A Western Gazette reporter is said to have gone to the scene and "witnessed the devastation". He was briskly directed to a spokesman for the United States Forces, in an office at Priory House, Greenhill, Sherborne. "Some forty" was then given as the death toll and he was told it was the largest single loss since American serviceman had arrived in England – this was a few weeks before the Slapton Sands debacle caused by E-boats off Portland.

The reporter filled a story with the Regional Censor at Bristol but only brief details made it into print, apparently some time later, as having happened "somewhere in the West Country".

The sadness for those on the frontline in the Dorset countryside was that their new found American friends would suddenly be taken from them. Action would be imminent the moment they were briefed and then kept behind the barbed wire of their camps. Such tearful separations happened not just at the end of May 1944 but for the whole of the rest of the year.

The bloody slaughter of the armada from Weymouth and Portland on Omaha Beach was at least an ending that was public and known but the fate of back-up troops for the clearance of the Germans from the Bretagne peninsula became a private grief.

The United States 262nd Infantry Division and part of the American 66th Division arrived on 26 November and left Piddlehinton Camp just before Christmas 1944. They sailed for Cherbourg with their ultimate objective being to clear the enemy out of the U-boat pens at Brest.

There would, however, be an attack on the Allied convoy in the English Channel and one large transport vessel was torpedoed, with considerable loss of life. The troopship *Leopoldville*, a Belgian passenger liner, was sunk on Christmas Eve by U-486 off Cherbourg, causing the death of 802 United States troops.

Not only was that incident as well covered-up as Slapton Sands but in a way it remains so to this day. "Probably a hundred of those chaps and their mates left Dorset girls with kids," one of their daughters told me. "It took me forty-five years to track down my father and find that he is alive in Ohio, but he won't acknowledge me as he has his own family and they don't know anything about me."

Piddlehinton Camp and its 802 death-toll deserve a special memorial for unveiling at Christmas in 1994. Whether it will get one is another matter.

Wartime **British Double Summer Time.**

Times in this book are given in the main in the 24-hour clock and are invariably British local time for the entries from the home front. British time was no longer the same as Greenwich Mean Time. On D-Day, for instance, British Double Summer Time was in force and had moved the clock forward by two hours. 00.00 (midnight) Greenwich Mean Time was therefore 02.00 hours British Double Summer Time and, to the enemy, it was 03.00 German Central Time.

CALENDAR 1944

(Leap Year)

January

S	.	2	9	16	23	30
M	.	3	10	17	24	31
Tu	.	4	11	18	25	..
W	.	5	12	19	26	..
Th	.	6	13	20	27	..
F	.	7	14	21	28	..
S	1	8	15	22	29	..

February

..	.	6	13	20	27	..	..
..	.	7	14	21	28	..	..
1	.	8	15	22	29	..	..
2	.	9	16	23	..	..	..
3	10	17	24	..	..	..	
4	11	18	25	..	..		
5	12	19	26	..	..		

March

..	5	12	19	26
..	6	13	20	27
..	7	14	21	28
1	8	15	22	29
2	9	16	23	30
3	10	17	24	31
4	11	18	25	..

April

S	.	2	9	16	23	30
M	.	3	10	17	24	..
Tu	.	4	11	18	25	..
W	.	5	12	19	26	..
Th	.	6	13	20	27	..
F	.	7	14	21	28	..
S	1	8	15	22	29	..

May

..	7	14	21	28	..
1	8	15	22	29	..
2	9	16	23	30	..
3	10	17	24	31	..
4	11	18	25	..	..
5	12	19	26	..	..
6	13	20	27	..	..

June

..	(4)	11	18	25
..	(5)	12	19	26
..	(6)	13	20	27
..	7	14	21	28
1	8	15	22	29
2	9	16	23	30
3	10	17	24	..

July

S	.	2	9	16	23	30
M	.	3	10	17	24	31
Tu	.	4	11	18	25	..
W	.	5	12	19	26	..
Th	.	6	13	20	27	..
F	.	7	14	21	28	..
S	1	8	15	22	29	..

August

..	6	13	20	27	..
..	7	14	21	28	..
1	8	15	22	29	..
2	9	16	23	30	..
3	10	17	24	31	..
4	11	18	25	..	..
5	12	19	26	..	..

September

..	3	10	17	24
..	4	11	18	25
..	5	12	19	26
..	6	13	20	27
..	7	14	21	28
1	8	15	22	29
2	9	16	23	30

October

S	1	8	15	22	29	..
M	2	9	16	23	30	..
Tu	3	10	17	24	31	..
W	4	11	18	25	..	..
Th	5	12	19	26	..	..
F	6	13	20	27	..	..
S	7	14	21	28	..	..

November

..	5	12	19	26	..
..	6	13	20	27	..
..	7	14	21	28	..
1	8	15	22	29	..
2	9	16	23	30	..
3	10	17	24	..	..
4	11	18	25	..	..

December

.	3	10	17	24	31
.	4	11	18	25	..
.	5	12	19	26	..
.	6	13	20	27	..
.	7	14	21	28	.
1	8	15	22	29	..
2	9	16	23	30	..

JUNE 1944

4 Sun—Trinity Sunday

Weymouth D-1 : Embark.

5 Mon

10 Sail : D. Day → France.
gales postponed.

6 Tues—Trinity Law Sittings begin
○ Full Moon

D+I   D: H 0645
Off the beach at last. 4.30pm

COLEVILLE - SUR - MER in view.

7 Wed

D+2 D+1
Tough going + under fire
Making S/E towards River Anne in sight

1944. Calendar and page from the diary of an unknown GI (an American 'General Infantryman') of the
Fighting Firsts, as the United States First Infantry Division were known.

1943-44. Burton Cliff, Burton Bradstock. Eyes towards France as American GIs turn south Dorset into a colossal armed camp and prepare to take the war back across the Channel.

D and H **Military abbreviations.**

In Army parlance, 'D' stands for the date scheduled for a big operation, and 'H' for the time at which offensive action is to start. This is expressed as 'H-hour'.

In terms of the invasion of Europe, D was set during the forward planning stage for 31 May 1944. For tidal reasons this was then revised to Monday 5 June. The calendar for the operation was set out in terms of D minus for days before 5 June. For instance, a programme of air attacks due to be operation by D-7 would be set for Monday 29 May.

Actually, because adverse winds caused a 24-hour postponement, D would become Tuesday 6 June. Overnight airborne operations for D-1/D would take place on the night of 5-6 June. D+6 would be Monday 13 June, by which date reinforcements were intended to bring the total invasion force to thirteen divisions, excluding airborne formations.

H-hour on the day ultimately chosen, Tuesday 6 June, would vary between 06.30 for the Western Task Force, to 06.45 on Omaha Beach, and 07.45 on the eastern sector of Juno area. For the first wave of airborne forces, in gliders from Tarrant Rushton, the coup de main – the military term for a sudden attack – would take place at 02.00 hours with the landing of Horsa gliders near Benouville.

1943-44. Burton Bradstock. Village boy mans A. E. Cheney's pumps, the Red House Garage, as another cleans the windscreen of an American jeep. Either side it is still pastoral Dorset.

1943-44. Burton Bradstock. Petty Officer Podger, recently invalided out of the Royal Navy after serving through both wars, points the way to the canteen for American GI Roy St Jean of Springfield, Massachusetts.

1943-44. Burton Bradstock. Cocoa, in NAAFI cups, bridges another generation gap. Corporal David W. Roberts, from Iowa, leans out of his holiday camp billet to chat with Betty 'Freckles' Mackay, a London evacuee from the Blitz days, and local boy Chris Kerley.

1943-44. Burton Bradstock. The propaganda of this superb series of pictures was every bit as good as the photography – here the subtle inference is that before 1783 Britain and America share a common history. The rector, Rev Arthur Dittmer, points to the inscription on one of his table-tombs.

1943-44. Burton Bradstock. St Mary's church, from the Rectory lawn. Tea is hosted by Rev and Mrs Arthur Dittmer and their tabby cat. Their United States Army guests (also seen opposite) S.M. Lieutenant S. M. Weitzner (left in this picture, right opposite) of Ridgewood, New York, and Major E. M. Beebe of Burlington, Vermont.

1943-44. Burton Bradstock. Blacksmith Benjamin Burton displays a hoof to the Americans. 'US troops are discovering that the Britisher is not as stand-offish as he is said to be' reads the contemporary caption.

1943-44. Burton Bradstock. 'Under the sycamore tree on the village green, a group of US soldiers talk to their friends the village children, and examine a machine-gun belt the children found on the beach.' The troopers are John L. Lawson of Port Jervis, New York; Robert S. Hastings of Azusa, California; Leo H. Pearson of Springville, New York; Corporal Roland Henry of Holland, Pennsylvania.

1943-44. Burton Bradstock. Contemporary caption: 'In the village canteen Gunner Weightman of the British Army, an old habitué, hands round home-made cakes to Corporal James Flower of Walpole, Massachusetts, Private First-class Roy St Jean of Springfield, Massachusetts, and Corporal Allan Decker of Chicago.'

1943-44. Burton Bradstock. The GI offensive began with the public houses. Here they are in the Dove. Their pint was beer – darker but less potent than the rough cider of the locals. H. and G. Simonds also had a brewery at Blandford – but the prominence of 'Reading' makes it likely that the poster was brought into the picture for propaganda purposes, to make it seem that the invasion force was gathering further east. The other poster makes an appeal on behalf of Prisoners of War.

1943-44. Burton Bradstock, at the west end of Chesil Beach. Preparing for the evening at an open-air hair salon on a boulder in the shingle. An American Ranger battalion is billeted in seaside camps to the west and east of the former holiday village.

1943-44. Burton Bradstock. Contemporary caption: 'In 1940 the beach was guarded against invasion, first by Local Defence Volunteers, then by Home Guards. Today, with the tables turned, United States troops can spend their leisure hours on it. Sitting on a concrete blockhouse, behind which, Britain's amateur ill-armed soldiers were prepared to sell their lives dearly, Corporal Bert Markowitz of Astoria, New York City, plays his violin. Markowitz was a student at the University of Miami and played with the National Broadcasting Corporation as a studio musician. Listening to him is G.R. Miller of Louisville, Kentucky.'

1944

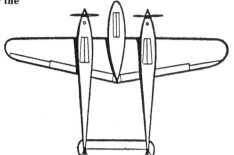

Lockheed P-38 Lightning: flown by the Americans from Warmwell.

March-August 1944. Markings of a Warmwell-based Lightning of the 428 Fighter Squadron of the Fighter Group of the United States Army Air Force.

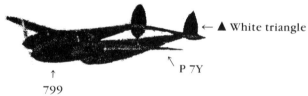

← ▲ White triangle

↑
799

↖ P 7Y

12 March 1944. Warmwell Aerodrome. American Lockheed P-38 Lightning fighter-bombers of the 474th Fighter Group bring a new shape to the south Dorset's sky.

"I AM NOW 50 YEARS OLD I PREFER A WAR NOW TO WHEN I AM 55..." – HITLER AUG. 23. 1939

20 April 1944. Cartoonists have a field day on the occasion of Adolf Hitler's fifty-fifth birthday. Der Fuhrer's words of 23 August 1939 are recalled. How right he is proving to be: 'I am now fifty years old. I prefer a war now to when I am fifty-five.'

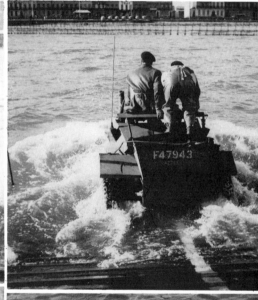

Early 1944. Weymouth Harbour. Opposite, top, 'Scam' project 'Swiss Roll' had a heavily laden Bedford lorry driving across the waves. The 'Scam' was to experiment publicly with projects that would be seen as applicable in seaborne landings against the fortified coast of north-eastern France, rather than the easier terrain of the Normandy beaches.

5 February 1944. Weymouth Bay. Opposite, four photographs. A Humber Scout car (bottom, left) drives into four feet of water off Weymouth promenade. It successfully drives through the sea (bottom, right). Next a Humber armoured car drives down the ramp of a tank landing craft (centre, left). And likewise a Daimler scout car.

5 February 1944. Weymouth Bay. The wading exercise continues. Weymouth's anti-invasion defences, dating from 1940, can be seen in the background of these shots. Perhaps the most amazing sight (top, right) was a Stuart tank travelling through six feet of water. Note the depth marker on its exhaust outlet. The other funnel carried air to the engine. Two other Stuarts pass in five feet of water (bottom, left). The timekeeper raises a flag to signal that the time limit of six minutes has expired (bottom, right)

5 January   Battered Flying Fortress makes it to Tarrant Rushton.

A flak-damaged B-17 Flying Fortress of the United States Army Air Force limped back across the Channel today after sustaining thirty hits over Mérignac airfield at Bordeaux.

The pilot proudly showed off his shell-shot bomber after he brought it down in a successful forced-landing at RAF Tarrant Rushton. He found himself among the gliders that are preparing for Exercise Nox. This is a major exercise that is to run for almost a week.

13 January   Military flying-boats return to Hamworthy.

RAF Hamworthy is operating flying-boats once more, this time as a station of 44 Group Transport Command. BOAC crews are flying on military secondment.

Their Sunderlands are tasked to operate to Karachi via Gibraltar, Tunis and Cairo, and will carry aircrew personnel who are needed in India and Burma.

14 January   Thirteen Tarrant Rushton Halifaxes cross the country.

Exercise Spook took place at Tarrant Rushton Aerodrome today; or rather it began there. Thirteen Halifax bombers of 298 Squadron practised long distance troop-carrying, to Winterton on the North Sea, where 115 men parachuted on to a dropping zone.

The Dorset aerodrome has also been busy, from 5 to 11 January, with Exercise Nox.

18 January   Montgomery finds his friends in Bridport.

"It is true you have made a score of enemies," General Bernard Montgomery was told by a friend when he returned to England, after visiting Prime Minister Winston Churchill in Marrakesh. "But you have made hundreds of thousands of friends as well."

He found them lining the streets when his mid-month tour of the 21st Army Group, brought together as the British invasion forces for the opening of the Second Front, had him being driven through Bridport. "Drive slowly," General Montgomery told his driver, as he saw that East Street was crowded with cheering civilians.

One lady pushed forward and succeeded in reaching his car, thanking him for the "wonderful job" he had done in North Africa and Italy. She then addressed a policeman who had tried to restrain her: "You cannot stop me from thanking the man who has saved this country!"

The general grinned broadly. He is returning to his old school, St Paul's at Hammersmith, which is his headquarters, and revising the top-secret "Cossac" plans for the invasion of Normandy. He first saw the details of Operation Overlord – of which he is overall land forces commander – whilst sitting beside Churchill's bed in Morocco on New Year's Day.

20 January   **Fog-bound Sunderland lands off Swanage.**

The coast of southern England was fog-bound as a Sunderland flying-boat came in from Gibraltar this morning. Flight-Lieutenant Satchwell did not receive a message that he was to divert from Poole Harbour to Pembroke dock in South Wales.

Instead, realising the impossibility of a harbour landing, he brought the Sunderland down into the sea four miles off Swanage. She was located by a launch from Poole which acted as pathfinder for the last ten miles of the journey. The flying-boat slowly taxied towards Poole for four hours and was put on its mooring at 13.20 hours.

20 January   **BOAC air-liner comes to Hurn.**

BOAC is transferring its land-planes – as distinct from the flying-boats operating from Poole Harbour – to RAF Hurn. A Mark I Lancaster transporter arrived today for evaluation as an air-liner in tests with a Development Flight unit.

G-AGJI has become the first civilian-flown Lancaster in Britain. It is without gun turrets though it retains wartime camouflage.

Trans-Canada Air Lines operate a similar converted bomber and BOAC is developing a specification for the manufacture of a version of the Lancaster for peacetime needs. Hitherto its solid-runway aircraft have been operating from Lyneham in Wiltshire.

Footnote The first of the post-war civilian Lancasters, to be known as the Lancastrian, was ordered in September 1944.

20 January   **Tarrant Rushton lifts off Canadians and tanks.**

Both specialities of airborne warfare were brought together at Tarrant Rushton Aerodrome today for Exercise Manitoba. It took its name from the participants. Firstly, eight Halifax aircraft of 298 Squadron carried the 1st Canadian Paratroop Brigade to a dropping zone. Then ten Halifaxes, from the same squadron, pulled Hamilcar gliders into the sky. These were loaded with Tetrarch Mark VII light tanks which just fit into a glider. They were released at a thousand feet.

Though now too thinly armoured for normal tank warfare, this 7.5 ton vehicle has a two-pounder gun and a 7.92-mm Besa machine gun, which were all that were necessary for taking on German tanks when it was made in 1939. In the scenario of an airborne landing it would hopefully be more likely to find itself in armoured reconnaissance or infantry support roles rather than facing the fire-power of front-line Panzers.

One Hamilcar and its Tetrarch overshot the landing area and split a Nissen hut apart as the tank shot forward from the debris. Both vehicle and driver survived.

26 January   **Halifax crashes beside Bournemouth Pier.**

Wreckage is being dragged ashore from a four-engined Halifax tug-plane, from RAF Hurn, which crashed today beside Bournemouth Pier.

28 January   Horsa glider lands on a wet flare-path.

Two disorientated Glider Regiment pilots of the British 6th Airborne Division were relieved to spot a double line of flares at 20.00 hours this evening. They proceeded to bring their Horsa glider down on to the flare-path of the western flying-boat 'trot' in the waters off RAF Hamworthy.

A BOAC Sunderland, waiting to take-off, radioed for a launch to come and take off the pilots. The glider, which had been released on a night-flying exercise, was then towed from the Wareham Channel by a BOAC pinnace and beached on the slipway at Hamworthy.

January   US Army hospitals built at St Leonards and Kingston Lacy.

An extensive General Hospital of the United States Army is being built on twenty acres of heathland to the south of the main road between Ferndown and St Leonards, near Ringwood. It is being prepared for use as a major surgical centre for casualties brought out of France after the planned invasion of Europe.

An extensive General Hospital is being established in the grounds of Kingston Lacy House at Pamphill, to the north-west of Wimborne.

January   Poole yards produce a landing craft a day.

Round the clock production in the three yards of shipbuilders J. Bolson and Son Limited at Hamworthy, Poole, brings about the completion of one assault landing craft a day. The LCAs are being tethered in Holes Bay. The yards, formerly the Skylark boat business which made yachts and other pleasure craft, also produce air-sea rescue speedboats and minesweepers, and carry out repairs on tank landing craft.

Work practises have been revolutionised. One squad is responsible for the complete production of a single vessel and this has helped Bolson's into their premier position – the largest assault landing craft manufacturers in Britain.

1 February   RAF Hurn and Tarrant Rushton are AEAF stations.

RAF Hurn and RAF Tarrant Rushton are among the many southern aerodromes where the Allied Expeditionary Force has an inter-service dimension. Joint service chiefs today presented the Supreme Commander, General Dwight D. Eisenhower, with their "Initial Joint Plan" at Bushy Park, Teddington, Middlesex, which is the Supreme Headquarters, Allied Expeditionary Force.

Hurn and Tarrant Rushton come under the RAF's 38 Group which is now part of the Allied Expeditionary Air Force, controlled from Stanmore, Middlesex, and Norfolk House in St James's Square. This is the headquarters of the Air Officer Commanding-in Chief, Air Chief

Marshal Sir Trafford Leigh-Mallory.

Likewise the 2nd Tactical Air Force of the RAF is working with the Second British Army, which includes the 6th Airborne Division, in the plans for Operation Overlord. British airborne troops are commanded by Lieutenant-General Frederick Browning, the husband of novelist Daphne du Maurier. Overall army strategy for the invasion of Europe is being prepared by General Sir Bernard Montgomery who has proposed an assault front comprising two armies with the First United States Army (two divisions) on the west flank and the Second British Army (three divisions, including the First Canadian Army) on the eastern side.

5 February   **Germans lose M156.**

Enemy boat M156, a Minensuchboot or minesweeper, is effectively out of the war for some time to come having been seriously damaged last night in a lengthy engagement with British destroyers HMS *Brissenden, Tantside, Talybont* and *Wensleydale*. She has been towed by a Vichy French craft into the estuary of Aber-Vrach.

Footnote M156 was still not safe; at Aber-Vrach she was further damaged by bombs from Coastal Command, Calshot.

5 February   **Amphibious landings on Weymouth sands.**

The 1940 invasion defences provided an authentic backdrop today to the bizarre spectacle of a practice attack by the most unseaworthy collection of craft ever to beach on Weymouth sands. They arrived in a fleet of LTCs, tank landing craft, and splashed down the ramps to wade ashore. The vehicles had to reach land in six minutes. The sea was obligingly flat.

9 February   **Twenty flotillas planned for Portland and Weymouth.**

Between them, Weymouth and Portland harbours could provide accommodation for a total of twenty flotillas of assorted landing craft for British assault Force G.

Held today at Portland Naval Centre, a top secret conference heard that the detailed preparations for Operation Overlord anticipate eleven flotillas of larger landing craft gathering at Portland and nine flotillas of assault landing craft at Weymouth.

12 February   **Leigh-Mallory visits Tarrant Rushton.**

Air Chief Marshal Sir Trafford Leigh-Mallory, Commander-in-Chief of the Allied Expeditionary Air Force, today visited Tarrant Rushton Aerodrome. He saw preparations for airborne landings and also relevant German aircraft equipment which has been assembled at the station to show flying crews some of the enemy's methods and ideas.

Tarrant Rushton hosts No.38 Group, Airborne Forces, which was formed from No.38 Wing, Army Co-Operation Command, on 11 October 1943. Its headquarters are at Netheravon, Wiltshire.

23 February   **King George visits the 1st Dorsets.**

His Majesty the King today visited the 1st Battalion of the Dorsetshire Regiment who are undergoing training at Halstead, Essex. He watched a company attack on a strongpoint supported by an assault pioneer platoon under Lieutenant W.F. Scott.

February   **Eisenhower and Monty at Bournemouth's Carlton Hotel.**

The Carlton Hotel on Bournemouth's East Cliff is one of the perquisites of the United States Army's occupation of this holiday coast – they would call it a perk. It is host to the American Forces Bureau of Investigation and some crews of self-propelled guns but still manages to rise to the occasional moments of style.

General Dwight D. Eisenhower, Supreme Commander Allied Forces Western Europe, and General Sir Bernard Montgomery, effectively commander-in-chief Allied land forces, though there is no such formal title, have used its facilities and the convenient clifftop view of rehearsals for invasion taking place in the bay below.

These, sadly, have not been without their casualties including soldiers aboard several Valentine DD [Duplex-Drive] tanks which are both amphibious and land vehicles; failings in their 'skirts' whilst carrying out the former role being the cause of the sinkings. These swimming tanks have canvas screens and propeller shafts at the rear. Hundreds of Shermans are being converted into DD tanks for the invasion assault.

Landing craft are now everywhere around, including the bays of Poole Harbour, Christchurch Harbour, and the inlets of the Solent such as Beaulieu River which also conceals the sunken sections of Mulberry Harbours. Most of the sand for making the caissons have come from pits at Stephen's Castle, Verwood.

February   **Massive airfield expansion at RAF Hurn.**

The two main runways at RAF Hurn have been increased in length by half as much again and a square mile of heathland on the north and east sides has been churned into a moonscape of yellow sand, crossed by the curves and frying-pan shapes of a complex network of dispersal areas.

These are being prepared for an armada of day and night-fighters, transport aircraft, tugplanes and gliders.

1 March   **644 Squadron formed at Tarrant Rushton.**

Personnel transferred from 298 Squadron, under the interim command of Squadron Leader A.G. Norman, have formed the new 644 Squadron at Tarrant Rushton Aerodrome. As with their parent squadron they will fly Halifax tug-planes with glider combinations in an airborne assault role.

7 March   **American flyers take over Station 416, ALG Christchurch.**

A temporary wire-mesh runway has been laid across the grass at

Christchurch Aerodrome which is now an Advanced Landing Ground. It is Station 416 of the 9th United States Army Air Force. Nearly a thousand officers and men of the 405th Fighter Bomber Group have begun arriving by train from Liverpool.

They disembarked from the liner *Mauretania* which had sailed from New York on 27 February. She cruised at 25 knots, without escorts, and changed her course every seven minutes "to prevent U-boats getting a head on her".

P-47 Thunderbolts of 509, 510 and 511 Squadrons of the United States Army Air Force will begin arriving next week.

9 March   **More Anti-Aircraft Squadrons to guard Tarrant Rushton.**

In view of its growing importance and use, the protection of Tarrant Rushton Aerodrome has been reinforced with the arrival today of the main body of 2733 Anti-Aircraft Squadron of the RAF Regiment from North Weald. Their advance party arrived in Dorset on 2 March.

The advance unit of another Anti-Aircraft Squadron, No. 2819 from Marston Moor, arrives on 11 March with its main body to follow on the 13th.

12 March   **Tragedy mars Warmwell's welcome for the Yanks.**

15.00 hours. Tragedy has ended a flying display put on by four RAF Typhoons of 263 Squadron to welcome the 474th Fighter Group of the United States Army Air Force on their arrival at the former Battle of Britain aerodrome at Warmwell. One of the four RAF planes spun out of a low roll and crashed half a mile west of the field. The pilot of HHS MN 129, Pilot Officer Graham Smith, was killed.

The Americans have designated Warmwell as Station 454. The are flying the strangest shape in the sky, the distinctive 400 mile per hour Lockheed P-38 Lightning fighter. The Luftwaffe call this aircraft the "fork-tailed devil".

14 March   **Hurn changes hands as Albemarles leave.**

RAF Hurn has been transferred to No.11 Group, Air Defence of Great Britain – as Fighter Command is now called – and its three squadrons of Albemarle troop and glider transports have left.

295 and 570 Squadrons have flown to Harwell and 296 Squadron has been redeployed to Brize Norton. Last month they flew supply drops from Hurn to the Resistance forces in occupied France.

Group Captain W.E. Surplice is Hurn's station commander.

17 March   **Canadian Typhoons and Hurricanes fly into Hurn.**

143 Wing of 83 Group of the 2nd British Tactical Air Force flew into RAF Hurn today. They are Canadian, with the Typhoons of 438 and 440 (Royal Canadian Air Force) Squadrons, and are to be joined by

Hurricanes of 439 (RCAF) Squadron. They will be dive-bombing targets in northern France.

RAF Fighter Command is being renamed Air Defence Great Britain, as the defensive arm of the service, with the Tactical Air Force taking on cross-channel offensive operations.

20 March   Mines exercise kills 29 Americans in Sherborne Park.

The 294th Engineer Combat Battalion of the United States Army lost twenty-nine men today in an accident at Sherborne. A live minefield had been laid in a training exercise in Sherborne Park which has an extensive American Camp on the ridge half a mile north-west Haydon.

On completion of the practices for the day the mines were gathered and stacked on a truck. This then slipped backwards. It activated one of the mines and the truck-load burst apart in a colossal explosion which ripped through C Company.

The dead are named as Sergeant Donald J. Walsh, T/5s Francis X. Gallagher, Warren F. Rapp, and Lawerence C. Sbaratta, Privates First Class Francis J. Murphy and Martin A. Norton, and Privates Charles W. Brinkofski, Robert M. Bucella, Edward D. Chiarieri, Anthony Cutrone, John P. Deevy, John W. Gadek, Robert Gladen, Jr., George E. Gundy, Harry B. Hanschka, Joseph B. Henning, Leonard B. Kerr, Stephen E. Kosiorowski, Roger E. Kroeger, Leo A. Lyon, John J. McHugh, Thomas S. Nicol, Lucien P. Pessoz, Conrad Propp, Robert L. Ready, Anthony T. Russo, Andrew Ter Waarbeek, Fred C. Tracey, and Joseph J. Zanelli.

21 March   Tyneham radar foils an E-boat incursion.

An attempt last night by the German 9th Schnellboot Flotilla to carry out a raid in Weymouth Bay was foiled by the radar apparatus at Brandy Bay, Tyneham, which with that on Portland Bill was able to correlate the movements of the enemy craft.

As a result the gun-laying by the coastal batteries of the Royal Artillery, from Swanage and Upton Fort at Osmington, into the sea off St Alban's Head, was so accurate that S84 collided with S139 as the attack was abandoned in disarray.

21 March   Hurn dog-fight ends in death crash.

Hurricanes of 439 (Royal Canadian Air Force) Squadron, flying since January from Wellingore, Lincolnshire, returned today to the skies above RAF Hurn, the station where they had been formed. Two American Thunderbolts were unable to resist the temptation of joining their dog-fights.

As Hurricane LD972 levelled off from a manoeuvre it was hit by one of the Thunderbolts, which ripped off the end of the Hurricane's wood and canvas starboard wing.

Though Flight-Lieutenant Norval E. Pollock was able to pull his damaged Hurricane out of an initial spin he then completely lost control, spiralling to his death in the Avon valley, two miles east of Hurn.

22 March **Nine die as Hurn Halifax crashes on Moordown.**

The seven-man crew of Halifax JP137 and two civilians were killed at 00.35 hours this morning when the bomber crashed in open ground below Meadow Court flats on the east side of Wimborne Road in the Bournemouth suburb of Moordown. It had lifted off from RAF Hurn, a mile and a half to the north-east, three minutes earlier.

Either the heavily-loaded four-engine Halifax failed to gain enough height to clear the Bournemouth plateau or the pilot, twenty-year-old Dennis Evans, had gathered insufficient speed and the aircraft stalled. It had come from 1658 Conversion Unit and was on a flight that would have delivered it to an RAF base in North Africa.

The crash could have been much more disastrous for the people of Moordown. Fortunately, there were no bombs aboard, though the plane was fully tanked with fuel and carried a cargo of ammunition and medical supplies.

It very nearly crashed on a densely-populated section of Moordown's main road. As it lost height the aeroplane clipped debris from the tops of Willis's builders-yard, the former tram depot, and a house in Malvern Road. This caused the aircraft to ricochet above the home of Mr and Mrs Claw and family before diving into the ground beside the garages to Meadow Court. Both wings were ripped off and the corner of the main building was struck, killing Mrs D. Bennett in flat number 9.

The fuselage and the tail rolled over on to the brick wash-houses behind two pairs of Victorian cottages next to the flats. Percy Chislett was killed in the centre cottage, 1027 Wimborne Road, but his wife and teenage son were able to escape from the exploding ammunition by scrambling out of the front bedroom window.

Sergeant Evans was from Middlesex and his navigator, 37-year-old Henry Roberts, from Cheltenham. Other crewmen were Flying Officer Stanley Appleton, aged 30, from Wembley; flight engineer Stanley Gent, 22, from Portslade; Sergeant George Alexander, whose age is not given, from Bedford; and Sergeant Reginald McGregor, 21, from New Westminster in British Columbia. The seventh man has not been identified.

23 March **Blandford AA gunners go to London.**

The American 184th Auxiliary Anti-Aircraft Artillery Battalion is on the move from Blandford Camp to London to supplement the capital's air defences. Its 'A' Battery has already left, having moved to Essex in January. It is feared the Germans will bombard London with flying bombs.

24 March **Top brass watch Tarrant Rushton mass take-off.**

The Halifax tug-planes of 298 Squadron at Tarrant Rushton Aerodrome today put on a showpiece take-off for the benefit of visiting top brass. Air Marshal Sir Douglas Evill had flown in earlier in the day with Air Commodore Francis Masson Bladin.

They watched as four Halifax aircraft, each towing a Hamilcar glider, prepared for a synchronised take-off. All four were airborne in a hundred seconds.

25 March   Seaplane saves 12 from glider sinking off Swanage.

A Walrus amphibian of 276 Squadron searched successfully for the glider of an airborne forces unit that came down in the sea today six miles south of Swanage.

The twelve men aboard were rescued and the Walrus then taxied on the surface for thirty minutes into Swanage Bay. There the soldiers were transferred to a launch.

25 March   Mosquitoes fly into Hurn to defend the night skies.

Mark XVII Mosquito night-fighters have flown into RAF Hurn from Valley in Anglesey. They are with 125 (Newfoundland) Squadron and will be controlled by Starlight, as Sopley radar is codenamed, in defensive interceptions over central southern England.

March   Pluto is laid across Poole Bay.

Pluto, the acronym of Pipe Line Under The Ocean, has been laid by the Tweedledrum, a great drum with cone-shaped ends, pulled by HMS *Conundrum* and a tug across twelve miles of Poole Bay to the Isle of Wight. This experiment by the Petroleum Warfare Department is to prove the feasibility of laying an underwater pipeline from a pumping station at Shanklin on the Isle of Wight across the English Channel to the proposed invasion beaches on the coast of Normandy.

March   'Scam' projects tested in Dorset.

The boffins are trying out their Scam Projects on the Dorset coast. A floating airfield, codenamed Lily, has been tested in Studland Bay by a Royal Navy Swordfish biplane carrying a bomb load and using rockets to enable the exceedingly short take-off.

'Scam' is the fun side of the secret war, experimenting publicly with projects of deception, that can be seen as applicable in seaborne attacks against the strongly fortified coast of north-eastern France – rather than the soft sands on Normandy.

For the Army there is a floating pier, the Swiss Roll, which has carried heavily laden Bedford lorries across Weymouth Harbour. More practical are the rockets being used to fire grapnels attacked to rope ladders for commandos to scale the 150-feet cliffs between Bridport and Burton Bradstock.

March   Swanage Great War VC passes on his experience.

Chief Petty Officer Ernest Pitcher of Swanage, who won the Victoria Cross in 1917 for staying at his gun in the classic action between an armed merchantman, a Q-boat, and a submarine, is back in uniform in this war at the age of fifty-seven. He rejoined in 1939 and is now training naval gunnery ratings.

Footnote Pitcher died in Gosport in 1946.

4 April   Warmwell airman saves drowning child.

Corporal Jerry Liroff, an off-duty American serviceman from the 474th Fighter Group at Warmwell, dived fully clothed into the sea off Plymouth today to rescue a drowning child.

7 April   Hurn Mosquitoes on the sidelines as Window opens to the sea.

Canadian Mosquito night-fighters of 125 (Newfoundland) Squadron from RAF Hurn have been flanking, at a wide distance, the twenty-five Lancaster and Stirling bombers involved in Exercise Eric. The bombers flew a circuit from Brighton inland to Stockbridge, on the Hampshire Downs, and then across the New Forest to Lymington.

Here, in the radar hole on German screens that is created by the Isle of Wight, they dropped strips of metallised paper, codenamed Window. This creates deceptive radar images.

The object of the exercise is to practice the dropping of Window in a manner that would suggest to a radar operator that a convoy is approaching steadily at about seven knots. There will have to be a long series of orbits that gradually overlap and which edge towards the enemy coast for a period of five hours. Precision flying will be required to create the illusion of ships rather than aircraft, and the paper will have to be dropped in bundles to simulate objects of the required size.

Footnote Over a hundred aircraft would take part in the actual deception, in the early hours of 6 June, including two squadrons of Lancasters. One was 617 Squadron of Dambuster fame. The feint was intended to make the enemy think that the D-Day landings were taking place in the area of Boulogne (Operation Glimmer) and Cap d'Antifer (Operation Taxable) though the Germans went one better than this and thought the invasion was much further east in the Pas de Calais.

Small naval craft, reflector balloons, and 'Moonshine' electronic devices were also deployed to complete the elaborate diversion the Stirlings of No. 3 Group Bomber Command dropped dummy parachutists and machines that emitted the sounds of mock-battle.

11 April   Christchurch Thunderbolts visit France.

Fifty-five P-47 Thunderbolts of the 405th Fighter Bomber Group of the United States Army Air Force today took off from Christchurch Advance Landing Ground. They assembled fighting formation at 20,000 feet over the English Channel and went on their first day trip to France.

The low-risk sweep of north-western France was intended to familiarise the pilots of 509, 510 and 511 Squadrons with the geography and some of the potential targets of the forthcoming offensive war. All the Thunderbolts returned safely.

14 April   Air-Sea Rescue Squadron drafted to Warmwell.

Another RAF squadron has returned to Warmwell Aerodrome, which is the base for forty-eight P-38J Lightnings of the American 474th Fighter Group.

275 (Air-Sea Rescue) Squadron flies Spitfires in coastal patrols, with an Anson to drop dinghies and a Walrus seaplane for pick-ups beyond the reach of a launch from Lyme Regis, Weymouth, Portland or Poole.

16 April   British Force G makes way for American Force O.

Though expected to gather in Portland and Weymouth for Operation Overlord, British invasion Force G has been relocated eastwards to the harbours and inlets of the Solent and Southampton Water.

Instead the Dorset ports are being allocated to United States Force O. They are destined for what is designated as Omaha Beach and the British troops are to land in the next sector to the east, codenamed Gold Beach.

Today Captain J.J. McGlynn of the United States Navy takes up his post as Commanding Officer United States Navy Advanced Amphibious Base Portland and Weymouth. This includes the three hards at Portland and HMS Grasshopper, the Royal Navy shore-base at Weymouth, plus ancillary facilities.

Captain McGlynn will be responsible for the embarkation of V Corps of the First United States Army which comprises the 1st US Infantry Division, 2nd US Infantry Division, 2nd US Armored Division, and two Ranger battalions.

The Fighting Firsts, as America's famous First Infantry Division is known, has its Divisional Headquarters at Langton House, Langton Long Blandford. The Commanding General, Major-General Clarence R. Huebner, has at his command 34,142 men and 3,306 vehicles.

It is estimated that there must now be a total of 80,000 American soldiers who are billeted in Dorset.

Bournemouth has been occupied by a succession of units that form the 3rd Canadian Division. Currently the town's hotels are taken over by the 8th Canadian Brigade which comprises the Queen's Own Rifles of Canada, Le Regiment de la Chaudiere, and the North Shore Regiment from New Brunswick. The headquarters is the Lynden Hall Hydro in Boscombe.

17 April   Two killed as Halifax crashes at Tarrant Rushton.

Two Halifax tug-planes of 644 Squadron are tasked tonight for an operation over France but the shock for the squadron came earlier when a routine take-off when wrong.

Halifax 'E' stalled and flopped on to the end of the runway, killing the pilot and the rear gunner. It had a glider in tow, but its crew were unhurt.

18 April   **King watches Exercise Smash assault Studland.**

The 1st Battalion of the Dorsetshire Regiment has been back on its native heath taking part in the repeated mock-invasion assaults of Exercise Smash across the sands of Studland Bay. Unlike normal exercises this one has been distinguished by the widespread use of live ammunition, from small-arms fire to bombs and rockets, and has been studied intently by high ranking officers and a succession of war lords.

From a massive concrete bunker, the Fort Henry observation post built by Canadian engineers on Redend Point, a row of field glasses has lined the slit that looks northward across Studland Bay and the whole of its beach.

Users of binoculars have included His Majesty King George VI, Prime Minister Winston Churchill, General Dwight D. Eisenhower (Supreme Commander Allied Expeditionary Force), General Sir Bernard Montgomery (effectively, for the assault, commander-in-chief Allied land forces, commanding the British 21st Army Group), General Omar Bradley (commanding the First United States Army), and Lieutenant-General Miles Dempsey (commanding the Second British Army).

The King's visit today was especially loud, being arranged to coincide with a demonstration of aerial carpet or pattern bombing. The royal train, bringing Churchill and Montgomery as well, arrived in Swanage.

Then Police toured the town and eastern Purbeck to warn people to open all their windows – to minimise the blast damage as the ground shook to the concussive thud of Studland's war.

Afterwards the King and the generals will dine in Swanage at the Grosvenor Hotel.

19 April   **Montgomery inspects units at Bovington Camp.**

The Driving and Maintenance Wing of the Armoured Fighting Vehicles School at Bovington Camp was today inspected by General Sir Bernard Montgomery, the overall land-force commander of Allied armies in western Europe. He came to Wool in his own train, the 'Rapier'.

19 April   **Bournemouth coast guns in action.**

Royal Artillery coast defence batteries at Hengistbury Head, Mudeford and the Needles opened up last night on the German 5th Schnellboot Flotilla as they laid magnetic mines in the eastern parts of Poole Bay and off the Isle of Wight.

S64 and S133 of the 8th Schnellboot Flotilla were damaged in a separate engagement last night when a Hunt-class destroyer, HMS *Whitshead*, caught up with them in foul weather.

22 April   **Eisenhower and Leigh-Mallory at Tarrant Rushton.**

General Dwight D. Eisenhower, the Supreme Commander of British and Allied Forces in western Europe, today flew into Tarrant Rushton Aerodrome to see the readiness of the British 6th Air Landing Brigade and its associated 6th Airborne Division.

He was accompanied by Air Chief Marshal Sir Trafford Leigh-Mallory, Commander-in-Chief of the Allied Expeditionary Air Force, and by Air Vice Marshal Leslie Hollinghurst.

They addressed air crews in the station briefing room. Tarrant Rushton houses over seven hundred men of 298 and 644 Squadrons, and 'C' Squadron of the Glider Pilot Regiment.

22 April   Warmwell's Lightnings sweep Brittany.

Forty-eight Lightnings of the 474th Fighter Group of the United States Army Air Force, from Warmwell, carried out a three-hour sweep across Brittany today in their first combat air patrol. All the planes returned safely.

22 April   York transport flies from Hurn to Cairo.

Avro York transport MW103, in wartime camouflage but manned by a British Overseas Airways Corporation crew, has taken off from RAF Hurn.

Based on the Lancaster wing and power-plant, with a new fuselage and tail assembly, it is destined to make the inaugural flight on a service to Morocco and along the southern Mediterranean to Cairo. Most, however, will be used as VIP transports and flying conference rooms.

24 April   Two dead in Bournemouth fire-attack.

Incendiary and phosphorus bombs fell at about 02.17 hours and damaged 156 Bournemouth properties – in Stour Road, Avon Road, Gresham Road, Strouden Road, Beatty Road, Portland Road, Charminster Road, West Way, Malvern Road, Shelbourne Road, and Holdenhurst Road. Two people are dead and seven injured.

Footnote The town's last bombs would be incendiaries dropped around the Roxy Cinema in Holdenhurst Road on 27 May 1944.

Bournemouth's wartime casualties totalled 219 dead and 507 injured, from 2,272 bombs of all types. Seventy-five properties were destroyed by direct hits, 171 were so badly damaged that they had to be demolished, and 13,345 required repairs; the vast majority only to windows and replacing slates.

24 April   Three killed in Poole incendiary attack.

Houses were damaged last night in an incendiary attack on the northern parts of Poole and Broadstone. Three people were killed, including firewatcher Arthur Martin, aged 59. Many fires were started but almost all were brought swiftly under control, leaving only thirteen people without homes.

Footnote B.T. Condon recalled the night for me, in 1987: "I was home on leave from the RAF. When the sirens sounded I decided to go down to the

ARP Wardens' Post in the annexe of the Broadstone Hotel to see if I could be of any help to my former ARP colleagues. My way took me past Willis the builders' merchants shop at the side of which was the lorry entrance to their paint store behind it. There I saw Mr Bryant, one of Willis's lorry drivers who lived nearby, and he asked for my help in reeling out a small hosepipe to fight a fire which had been started in the paint store."

"Imagine our dismay when we found that we could get no water through the tap, presumably because the Fire Service were using all the main supply elsewhere. Some of the bombs dropped on that occasion were fiendish 'Ibsens' [Incendiary Bomb Separating Explosive Nose]. These were designed with a delayed action fuse on an explosive device which separated from the fire-bomb on impact and exploded shortly afterwards with the object of maiming anyone fighting the fire caused by the incendiary."

24 April   Hurn Mosquitoes claim three Ju88s.

Last night eight Mosquito night-fighters of 125 (Newfoundland) Squadron of the Royal Canadian Air Force, flying from RAF Hurn, intercepted a formation of Junkers Ju88 bombers. All the fighters returned safely to the station, with claims that they had shot down three of the bombers, and that two others had been damaged.

25 April   American AA gunners arrive at Gillingham.

Sandley House is the headquarters for the 554th Anti-Aircraft Artillery Battalion of the United States Army which is now billeted at Gillingham.

The house, between Gillingham and Buckhorn Weston, stands immediately above a tunnel which carries the Waterloo-Exeter railway line beneath its grounds. The low hill now bristles with guns.

26 April   'Moving targets' constructed on Kimmeridge cliffs.

Training for the Sherman tank crews of the American 2nd Armored Division has become more sophisticated with the construction of a series of moving targets that are winched along narrow-gauge railway tracks.

The winching wires are protected by stout embankments. Targets spring up behind them and can move and stop like vehicles. Shells harmlessly overshoot the clifftop and fall in the sea.

This range has been created at Swalland Farm, east of Kimmeridge, and extends in six zig-zag sections from a point west of Clavell's Hard to midway between Rope Lake Head and Swyre Head. The main tank gunnery ranges are on the other side of the village, extending to Lulworth, having been massively expanded by the inclusion of Tyneham parish and other lands on 19 December 1943.

28 April   Six hundred Americans massacred off Portland.

Last night a convoy of eight American tank landing ships [LSTs], sailing west from the Solent for the big Exercise Tiger practice landings at Slapton Sands, Devon, were intercepted by E-boats as they rounded Portland Bill to enter Lyme Bay.

Motor torpedo boats of the 5th and 9th Schnellboot Flotillas ran amok amongst the Americans off the Portland end of the Chesil Beach, which is known locally as Dead Man's Bay, so-called in the works of Thomas Hardy from the memory of earlier shipwreck calamities .

A total of 441 United States soldiers have been killed or drowned, together with 197 seamen; LST507 and LST531 are sunk with the loss of twelve tanks; LST289 is damaged by a torpedo.

The coastal gun batteries at Blacknor Fort, Portland, prepared to open fire, but the American commander ordered them not to do so, in view of the number of his men who were in the water.

The E-boats withdrew on the arrival of a corvette, HMS *Azalra,* and HMS *Saladin.* They were then joined by HMS *Onslow.*

Footnote The dead would be stacked in piles on Castletown Pier in Portland Naval Dockyard. Offshore, teams of Navy divers worked for days to recover the identity discs from the other bodies, to account for all the missing and give Allied Naval Headquarters the welcome news that none had been fished out alive from the sea by the Germans and taken prisoner. Confirmation of their demise was accompanied by immense feelings of relief. "This cloud's silver lining," as it was put in a secret memorandum, was the assurance that the invasion plans were still secret.

30 April   RAF Hamworthy closes.

The short direct connection with military flying-boats has ended at Poole with the closure of RAF Hamworthy.

Service flying-boats can, however, still be refuelled and oiled at Poole by BOAC.

30 April   Thunderbolt crashes in Highcliffe School playground.

19.03 hours. Police confirm an aircraft has crashed near the Globe Inn, Lymington Road, Highcliffe. Christchurch ARP have had a report of a parachute descending south-east of Hoburne House.

19.20. Damage reported to two houses in Woodland Way.

19.25. Report of damage to Highcliffe School and the ARP store there, as well as water-mains fractured. A rescue party is being sent from Sandhills depot.

19.35. The aircraft crashed in the playground at Highcliffe School. It was a P-47 Thunderbolt of the 405th Fighter Bomber Group of the United States Army Air Force and had been preparing to land at Christchurch Advance Landing Ground. Its remains lie in a crater and pieces of metal and other debris cover the trees on the other side of the road.

19.40. The American pilot has landed unhurt in the nearby recreation ground.

Footnote Les White of Glenville Road, Walkford, recalls chatting with the 'Snowdrops' (US Military Police) at their road-block between Humphreys Bridge and SRDE (now Plesseys) as the Thunderbolts were landing. "Several were down when we noticed that one was circling at about 3,000 feet and as we watched we saw that the port wing was so badly damaged that it was visibly flapping. A coloured soldier came across the airfield on a bike and told the 'Snowdrops' that the pilot had decided to head out to sea and use his parachute.

"As we watched he baled out and the aircraft, now without any control, was caught by the stiff sea breeze and turned back inland. As my friend and I pedalled our bikes back towards Highcliffe we heard the thud of the crash and arrived on the scene to see the remains of the Thunderbolt lying in a shallow crater in the school yard."

April   83 Group has six offensive squadrons at Hurn.

Rocket-firing Hawker Typhoons of 181, 182 and 247 Squadrons, which form 124 Wing, are now at RAF Hurn. They bring to six the number of offensive squadrons at the airfield that comprise 83 Group of the 2nd British Tactical Air Force.

They are flying regular ground-attack missions across Brittany and Normandy. The rockets have their own propellant and fire clear of the aircraft without recoil. Eight are carried by each aircraft.

April–July 1944. Several squadrons of Hawker Typhoons fly from RAF Hurn, on rocket-firing ground-attack missions across the English Channel.

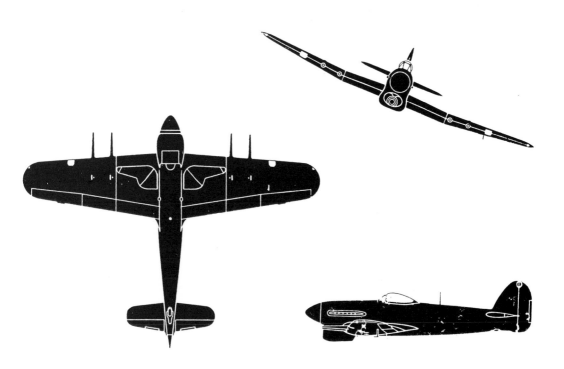

February 1944. Bournemouth. General Dwight D. Eisenhower and General Bernard Montgomery at the Carlton Hotel, making plans for the invasion of Europe. They had been watching assault landing rehearsals in Poole Bay.

Early 1944. Burton Bradstock. Rope ladders being fired by rockets from assault landing craft to the top of the 150 feet cliff. Grapnels are attached to the rockets. This is one of the better 'Scam' projects for invasion innovations.

Early 1944. Abbotsbury. Lighting up the night. Star shells fired from two-pounder Pom-poms illuminates the Channel in a 'Scam' project exercise. In that mass of light there are forty or more shells bursting. Silhouetted against the sea are the concrete anti-tank defences of the Chesil Beach, a reminder of the days when the invasion threat was in reverse.

March 1944. Studland Bay. One of the more bizarre 'Scam' projects was for a floating airfield, codenamed 'Lily'. It was tried out on a reassuringly flat sea, with a Swordfish 'Stringbag' biplane. The aircraft, heavily loaded, is about to use rocket assisted take-off gear to become airborne.

Early 1944. Hurn Aerodrome. The scale of the expansion is shown by the light areas of disturbed sand. All the dark, tarmac runways are new. North is at the top of the picture and the initial area of the base is shown by the light, concrete shade of the original perimeter taxiway.

1944. Knighton Heath Wood, beside Warmwell Aerodrome. United States Army Air Force tree-trunk graffiti, photographed in 1993 by Steven Murdoch.

1944. Christchurch Aerodrome. Opposite. American P-47 Thunderbolts of 510 Squadron of the USAAF's 405th Fighter Bomber Group, Lieutenant Curry Powell shows off his oomph-girl Ann Sheridan on 'Georgia Peach'. Lieutenant Charles Mohrle sits in 2Z-M 'Touch of Texas'.

April 1944. Above, Poole Harbour. A line of assault landing craft, built by Bolson's at Hamworthy and Poole, at anchor in Holes Bay. Production is running at one per day. Vast quantities of craft are accumulating in inlets and estuaries along the South Coast as central southern England prepares for the invasion of Europe.

Early 1944. Studland Beach. Tanks and beaches don't go well together. Failure (top, left) as the Churchill tank fails to climb one of the steeper parts of the sand dunes. So enter one of Hobart's Funnies (top, right). Major-General Percy Hobart of the 79th Armoured Division designed a series of ingenious machines that could ease the way for tanks, and however strange they looked, his vehicles were to save hundreds of lives in the Normandy campaign. Here, an AVRE lays a carpet from a bobbin, across the soft sand. Next, using the carpet that AVRE has laid, the Churchill tank repeats its attempt at climbing the dune (above, left). This time it disappears over the top (above, right). On the left-hand side of this picture you can see the deep rut left by its first, unaided, failure.

April 1944. Opposite. Slapton Sands, Devon. In exercise Fabius landing craft from Portland, Weymouth and Poole joined in the major dummy run for D-Day and the invasion of Normandy. Three tank landing craft are unloading in this sector, protected by barrage balloons from fighter attack.

March-August 1944. Lockheed P-38 Lightnings of the American 474th Fighter Group, flying from Warmwell, are now the commonest aeroplane in the sky over south Dorset.

April 1944. Opposite. The Union Jack will be taken across the channel, but first it is raised on Slapton Sands, Devon. Exercise Fabius is the major dummy run for D-Day.

1943-44. Studland. Fort Henry at Redend Point, Studland. One of Britain's most important relics of World War Two. Length 90 feet, concrete walls almost three feet thick, and recessed observation slit 80-feet long. From it the top brass watched live-fire rehearsals for the Normandy landings. Behind the field-glasses were the King, Churchill, Eisenhower and Montgomery, plus just about all their generals and aides. Post-war sycamores, spoiling the view of the sands, have been felled by the National Trust.

19 April 1944. Bovington Camp. General Sir Bernard Montgomery arrives as the overall land-force commander of Allied armies in the preparations for Operation Overlord visiting the Armoured Fighting Vehicles School, he is at home in his Royal Tank Corps beret. His mobile base, his own train – the 'Rapier' – is in a siding at Wool station.

April   **Americans bring death to Dorset roads.**

The increase that the United States Army has brought to traffic on Dorset's roads is reflected in this month's accident fatalities, which have risen to seven from only two in April 1943. Colonel Frederick R. Lafferty, the Provost Marshal of 7-Base Section of the US Army, is to instigate five military police patrol groups to control traffic flow at major junctions.

April   **Unexploded phosphorus bomb at Holton Heath.**

A five kilogram German bomb packed with phosphorus has failed to explode inside the Royal Naval Cordite Factory at Holton Heath. The contents have been steamed out and it is now on display as a trophy.

1 May   **Second Mosquito squadron comes to Hurn.**

604 (County of Middlesex) Squadron arrived today at RAF Hurn. They are the second Mosquito squadron at the station and are led by Wing Commander Gerald Maxwell.

5 May   **Hurn Mosquitoes claim two kills.**

Directed by Starlight, as the RAF's Sopley radar station is known, the Mosquitoes of 125 and 604 Squadrons were airborne last night. The Hurn-based night-fighters were successful in making a number of interceptions of Luftwaffe raiders.

125 Squadron claimed a Junkers Ju88 destroyed and a Messerschmitt Me410 damaged. 604 Squadron reported a Dornier Do217 shot down and a Junkers Ju88 damaged.

7 May   **Warmwell loses two Lightnings in France.**

Two American Lightnings from Warmwell, escorting B-26 Marauders into France, have been shot down. Lieutenants Merkle and Thacker are missing. The returning planes claimed one probable kill, a Focke-Wulf 190, which is little consolation. The station mood is grim.

Footnote Merkle was killed but Thacker was to surprise his colleagues by escaping into Spain and making it back to Warmwell in June.

13 May   **2nd Dorsets lose 75 men to recapture a piece of Burma.**

Having cost seventy-five Dorset lives in fierce fighting against the Japanese that has dragged on for three weeks, the 2nd Battalion of the Dorsetshire Regiment today achieved its costly objective and ousted the enemy from the Kohima Ridge; a second-class hill station at 5,000 feet in central Burma.

For the Japanese it is a major strategic disaster but for the West Countrymen it has been hell. Many of the Dorset dead have been left where they fell since 27 April.

The padre held a service on the tennis court near where 'C' Company had sustained the greatest losses in the initial attack. The men were joined by Richard Sharp of the BBC:

"We are still on the six hills in the centre of Kohima. We've mopped up nearly all the Japs on them, and we've taken the famous tennis court. A half-smashed bunker on one of the hills was giving us a good deal of trouble, but we took it at one [13.00 hours] today, and I've seen the hill myself. It's covered with dead Japs. I counted up to forty of them and then stopped. Our men have been sprinkling them with quicklime – a necessary precaution in this weather.

"The men who took it came from a battalion of a West Country regiment. They've been plugging away at that tennis court for sixteen days and they'd become personal enemies of the Japs there, who used to taunt them at dusk, calling across the tennis court: 'Have you stood-to yet?' Today they're on top and they walked on their toes, laughing, among the bulges in the earth of dug-out roofs; their muscles limber. ready to swivel this way or that in an instant.

"There was a company commander [Captain Clive Chettle], a robust man with a square, black jaw covered with stubble. The skin between his battle-dress trousers and his tunic was bloody, and he swayed as he stood with his legs straddled. But his brain was working at full speed, and he laughed and shouted to his men as they went eagerly from fox-hole to fox-hole with hand grenades and pole charges – that's twenty-five pounds of explosive at the end of a six-foot bamboo."

13 May   Eisenhower meets the 1st Dorsets.

The Supreme Commander Allied Forces, General Dwight D. Eisenhower, today visited the 231st Infantry Brigade who are training in the New Forest at Cadlands Camp, Fawley. Representatives of the 1st Battalion of the Dorsetshire Regiment were among those whose confidence he gained.

15 May   Junkers Ju188 shot down off Portland.

While on routine defensive patrol at midnight, a Beaufighter Mark VI night-fighter of 68 Squadron, from RAF Fairwood Common in the Gower peninsula, made visual contact with a high-flying bandit over the English Channel. The interception, at 25,000 feet, was brought about by radar from Hope Cove control, based in the hills above Salcombe, Devon. A single German reconnaissance aircraft was suspected; looking down on a Channel full of vessels with a big American fleet gathered off Portland.

The sighting was brought to a conclusion at 00.43 hours this morning. Beaufighter pilot Flying Officer Giblet Wild, and his observer, Flying Officer Frederick Baker, detail the kill of a Junkers Ju188 in their combat report:

"Bandit had been gently weaving during the chase. On closing in to 800 feet bandit was identified as a Ju188 by the oval-shaped nose, long pointed wings and tapering tailplane with single fin. From 25 yards range a 2-second burst of cannon was given and strikes were seen on the fuselage and port engine. We then got enemy aircraft's slipstream and dropped to port and below.

"On coming out with a slow starboard turn, we noticed that the bandit was turning slowly to port and falling. We closed in to 150 yards and gave a long burst, from dead astern, of about 4-seconds. Strikes were then seen on fuselage and starboard engine, which burst into a bright orange flame, spreading along the fuselage. Bandit then fell away vertically below fighter's port wing with flames growing larger and brighter.

"We then did a hard port turn and dived after bandit but by the time we got round the enemy aircraft fell into hazy cloud about 10,000 feet below, well ablaze. The time was then 00.43 and position some 35 miles south-south-west of Portland. As soon as bandit went down we gave 'murder' over the R.T. and understood that a fix was taken by Hope Cove at Z 0560.

"In view of the continuous succession of strikes and the size of the fire which was spreading throughout the aircraft and the fact that it appeared obviously out of control when it fell away, we claim one Ju188 destroyed. No window (radar-confusing foil) was seen, enemy aircraft was interrogated (asked to Identify Friend or Foe) three times on A.I. (Airborne Interception) set and gave no response. No return fire was experienced. No exhaust flames were seen."

The Beaufighter had taken off from Fairwood Common at 22.22 last night and returned at 01.30 this morning. Its four cannon mounted in the fuselage, had used a total of 767 rounds of 20mm ammunition, principally heavy explosive incendiaries. There had been no stoppages. The six smaller wing-mounted Brownings were not used.

Footnote This kill was confirmed on 17 May 1944 when wreckage was found by the Royal Navy. The combat report was sent to Rodney Legg by Beaufighter observer F.F. Baker, from retirement at Holme-next-Sea, Hunstanton, Norfolk, on 22 December 1991.

15 May   Zeals Mosquito shoots down Dornier.

A German raider which penetrated Dorset air space in the early hours this morning was tracked by radar along its northerly course, apparently towards Bristol. It was engaged by a Mosquito night-fighter of 488 (New Zealand) Squadron from Zeals Aerodrome, to the west of Mere, which was flown by Flying Officer Ray Jeffs, pilot, and Flying Officer Ted Spedding, the navigator.

Their target, a Dornier 217K, was picked up by Yeovil's searchlights and came into their sights as it crossed into Somerset. They raked it with fire. The Dornier's right-hand engine was blazing and it crashed into the countryside at West Camel.

The pilot, Johannes Domschke (20), died from his wounds but the crewmen, observer Emil Chmillewski (21), wireless operator Waldemar Jungke (22), and gunner Otto Schott (23), parachuted into captivity.

Opened in May 1942, RAF Zeals is a mile north-east of Bourton, which is Dorset's most northerly parish.

15 May   Four hurt by Purewell bomb.

Four casualties were rescued from Purewell Hill House, Christchurch, after it had been hit at 02.22 hours by a German bomb.

Another fell at West View, Stanpit, about the same time and damaged houses over a wide area. Bombs also dropped behind the OK Garage, Somerford, and at Woolhayes, Highcliffe. The latter failed to explode.

18 May   Mass glider exercises at Tarrant Rushton.

11.04 hours. Twelve Halifax-Hamilcar combinations of 298 Squadron, plus a further twelve of the same type of tug-planes and gliders from 644 Squadron, are lined up beside the main runway at Tarrant Rushton Aerodrome for a mass take-off.

19.00 hours. This morning's exercise is now to be repeated at Tarrant Rushton, this time with eighteen Halifax-Hamilcar combinations from each of the two squadrons, in order to give the pilots experience of mass take-offs and landings at dusk.

Similar large-scale practices will take place on 22 and 29 May.

21 May   American pilot killed at Cheselbourne.

An American pilot from Warmwell, Lieutenant Kimball, was killed when his Lightning fighter crashed near Cheselbourne.

21 May   Acoustic mine defused in Lyme Bay.

Lieutenant-Commander Bryant and Petty Officer Clark of the Royal Navy have defused one of the new-type acoustic pressure mines that the Germans have laid in Lyme Bay.

They were dropped from German Schnellboote S136, S138 and S140 on the night of 18 May.

Conventional mines have also been sown by Schnellboote S144, S130, S145, S146, S150 and S168 before three Royal Navy destroyers with three motor gun-boats, from Portland, forced their withdrawal to France.

22 May   Another Warmwell Lightning lost in France.

Lieutenant Usas, an American Lightning pilot from Warmwell, was killed in France whilst on a mission to dive-bomb a strategic target.

23 May   Two Junkers fall to Hurn's Mosquitoes.

Both the night-fighter squadrons based at RAF Hurn were operational over Southampton and Portsmouth last night.

604 Squadron failed to find the German bombers but nine Mosquitoes from 125 Squadron came upon them at 00.15 hours. Their first claim was a Junkers Ju88 that was shot down at 00.20, followed by another Ju88 damaged at 00.40. A third Ju88 was then engaged and seen to be crashing to the ground at 00.45.

25 May   **Wellington crashes at Christchurch.**

13.00 hours. An RAF Wellington bomber has crashed near Christchurch Aerodrome, on the north side of the railway line.

28 May   **Weymouth air-raid damages 400 houses.**

At 01.03 hours the air-raid sirens warbled at Weymouth but two minutes earlier the bombs had started to drop and they were to damage four hundred houses. Some hundred of them are badly smashed and fire has also damaged Weymouth Hospital and the Christian Science Church. Three Civil Defence volunteers and a junior ATS commander have been killed and thirteen of the injured have been detained in hospital.
    Patients from the Weymouth and District Hospital, hit by a bomb and with another still unexploded beneath it, have been evacuated by Colonel Knoblock and the Medical Corps of the United States Army to the Emergency Hospital established in Weymouth College.

Footnote The hospital bomb had buried itself twenty-eight feet in the ground and could not be reached and deactivated for several days.

28 May   **German mine-layers driven off.**

An attempt last night by the German 5th Schnellboot Flotilla to lay mines off the Dorset coast was seen off by Beaufighters from RAF Holmsley South in the New Forest aided by the Poole Bay coast defence batteries and Royal Navy destroyers from Portland and Portsmouth.
    The fleeing German boats used their speed to escape but all are taking home some damage.

30 May   **Mass glider moonlit take-off at Tarrant Rushton.**

Tonight a mass take-off of Halifax-Hamilcar combinations at Tarrant Rushton Aerodrome is to test the station's expertise at mounting an airborne operation in moonlight.

May   **Paddle-steamers lay hundreds of British mines.**

Requisitioned paddle-steamers have joined the mine-layer HMS *Plover* in laying one thousand two hundred mines in defensive barriers to protect the concentrations of invasion craft in Dorset and Hampshire estuaries from enemy E-boats.
    The Auxiliary Paddle Minesweepers *Medway Queen*, *Ryde*, *Whippingham* and *Sandown* and the 10th, 51st and 52nd Mine-Laying Flotillas have been carrying out the task under the watchful eyes of an assortment of escort vessels from the 9th, 13th, 14th, 21st and 64th Motor Torpedo Boat Flotillas.

Footnote These minefields were to claim the richest haul of Axis shipping in the in the channel of the whole war; 102 enemy vessels would be accounted for.

May   **Seven hundred Americans invade Charborough Park.**

A United States Army mechanised supply unit of seven hundred men with a hundred heavy six-wheeled vehicles has camped in Charborough Park and dug slit trenches against air attack. The only incident has been caused by a red stag that was nibbling grass and pushed its head into the side of a tent and a sleeping Yank.

The Americans, however, have swiftly developed a taste for young peafowl – not unlike turkey – and those from the Wild West are adept at throwing knives into the trunks of the cedar trees. Admiral Drax's staff have noticed that the Americans drive everywhere, even distances of a few yards, and there is hardly a lawn or patch of grass that isn't being worn bare.

4 June   **Montgomery: 'The time has come'.**

Message to all ranks of the 21st Army Group from its Commander-in-Chief, General Sir Bernard Montgomery: "The time has come to deal the enemy a terrific blow in Western Europe. To us is given the honour of striking a blow for freedom which will live in history."

4 June   **Invasion postponed, for 24 hours.**

21.00 hours. Wind speeds in the English Channel are predicted for the morning to be west-north-west Force Five [12 to 16 knots] with consequent mid-Channel waves six feet in height.

Hearing this, and that the wind should then back to west-south-west and slacken to Force Three to Four [7 to 15 knots] General Dwight D. Eisenhower and Admiral Sir Bertram Ramsay, meeting with their chiefs of staff in the library at Southwick Park, near Portsmouth, have postponed Operation Overlord for twenty-four hours.

4 June   **French battleship in difficulty off Bournemouth.**

22.00 hours. The D-Day postponed signal has been sent to anchorages and aerodromes across southern England. Some slower vessels were already at sea, such as the old French battleship *Courbet* which was being towed south of the Needles and made heavy going off Bournemouth.

Filled with concrete, she is a 'Gooseberry' blockship and is to be sunk off the Normandy coast. Meanwhile, with considerable difficulty, her tug has brought her into the lee of Durlston Head, Swanage, where she has dropped her 7-ton anchor.

As the engines and boilers have been stripped the great vessel has no power with which to weigh anchor tomorrow evening. The cable will therefore have to be slipped when she is due to be tugged to her final resting place.

5 June   **The invasion – it's on.**

04.00 hours. The Supreme Commander Allied Forces Western Europe, General Dwight D. Eisenhower, has given the order that the invasion of Europe is to take place tomorrow. It should have gone ahead today but has been postponed because of the heavy seas.

A lull is expected in the winds tomorrow but they are forecast to gather strength again in the evening.

This would rule out the 7th, the last day of present favourable tidal cycle, and it is therefore imperative that unless the entire operation is stood-down it must begin at midnight.

5 June   **American conference aboard 'Ancon' at Portland.**

There has been a dawn meeting aboard the United States Ship *Ancon* in Portland Harbour. She is the Command Post (Advanced) of Admiral John L. Hall and will be the headquarters craft off Omaha Beach for Leonard T. "Gee" Gerow who is in command of V Corps of the United States Army. USS *Chase* will stand by as Command Post (Alternative).

Major-General Clarence R. Huebner, those 1st Infantry Division is to land on Ohama Beach, has been joined by General Omar Bradley and Admiral Alan G. Kirk, in overall command of the naval invasion force.

Their consensus is that the operation should not be further postponed. "It will be disastrous to have troops cooped up on board for another two weeks," one of them said. Their message to General Eisenhower, which is being relayed by Admiral Kirk, is that the invasion should take place tomorrow.

5 June   **Americans forewarned of a 'chaotic' Omaha Beach.**

14.00 hours. Brigadier-General Norman D. Cota of the 29th Infantry Division has called a meeting of his staff in the wardroom of the United States Ship *Charles Carroll*, at anchor in Portland Harbour.

He warned his men: "This is different from any of the other exercises that you've had so far. The little discrepancies that we tried to correct on Slapton Sands are going to be magnified and are going to give way to incidents that you might at first view as chaotic."

"You're going to find confusion. The landing craft aren't going in on schedule, and people are going to be landed in the wrong places. Some won't be landed at all."

"We must improvise, carry on, not lose our heads."

5 June   **Three Warmwell pilots killed on the Seine.**

A cloud-base near ground level forced the Lightnings of the American 474th Fighter Group from Warmwell into the trees as they approached their target bridge over the River Seine.

Major Bedford, Lieutenant Coddington, and Lieutenant Temple were killed and several of the surviving planes brought back tree boughs in their tails.

28 May 1944. Weymouth. Melcombe Avenue as clearing up begins after what will turn out to be the town's last major air raid of the war.

Early in June 1944. Weymouth. Unexploded! Raising the hospital bomb.

Early 1944. Poole. Rocket-firing landing craft RCL (B) 640 being completed in Bolson and Son's yard.

1944. Tarrant Rushton. Training take-off for a troop carrying Horsa glider being lifted by a twin engine Albemarle tug-plane. Such a pair, one of three destined for the French coast at Merville, would be the first to take to the air on 5 June 1944, the eve of D-Day. That is to be a lift-off at dusk, and larger Halifax-Horsa combinations. The scene, photographed earlier in the day, appears in the unique sequence that follows. These were assembled jointly by Rodney Legg and Leslie Dawson, principally for the latter's 'Wings over Dorset' which has numerous personal stories from Tarrant Rushton in the run-up to 'the longest day'.

1 June 1944. South Dorset. V Corps of the First United States Army, including the 2nd Armored Division, is the county's army of occupation. It has gathered its tanks into vast fields of armour and the men file behind barbed wire for their briefings. From now on they are to have no conversations with civilians (the notice is at Puddletown; the lesser one reads–'In case of fire call N.F.S. [National Fire Service] Dorchester. Telephone Dorchester 766. You are at D3')

Weymouth Quay, above. The two black lads, Asa Jones and Furrell Browning from Dallas, man an anti-aircraft gun aboard USS 'Henrico'. The preparations for the D-Day embarkation's were to go unmolested.

4 June 1944. The message from General Bernard Montgomery, Commander-in-Chief Allied Land Forces. It is addressed to 'all Troops' in 21 Army Group, which comprises the First United States Army, the First Canadian Army, the Second British Army, airborne forces, continental contingents, and headquarters staff.

21 ARMY GROUP

PERSONAL MESSAGE FROM THE C-in-C

To be read out to all Troops

1.   The time has come to deal the enemy a terrific blow in Western Europe.

The blow will be struck by the combined sea, land, and air forces of the Allies—together constituting one great Allied team, under the supreme command of General Eisenhower.

2.   On the eve of this great adventure I send my best wishes to every soldier in the Allied team.

To us is given the honour of striking a blow for freedom which will live in history; and in the better days that lie ahead men will speak with pride of our doings.   We have a great and a righteous cause.

Let us pray that " The Lord Mighty in Battle " will go forth with our armies, and that His special providence will aid us in the struggle.

3.   I want every soldier to know that I have complete confidence in the successful outcome of the operations that we are now about to begin.

With stout hearts, and with enthusiasm for the contest, let us go forward to victory.

4.   And, as we enter the battle, let us recall the words of a famous soldier spoken many years ago :—

" He either fears his fate too much,
Or his deserts are small,
Who dare not put it to the touch,
To win or lose it all."

5.   Good luck to each one of you.   And good hunting on the mainland of Europe.

B. L. Montgomery

4 June 1944. Codename Phoenix (above). One of the 146 concrete caissons, of varying height and weighing between 1,500 and 6,000 tons, that will be towed across to Normandy to arrive on the top of tide on D+3, if weather conditions are suitable. They will be sunk on the offshore sands to form two huge prefabricated harbours, each the size of that at Dover. These are codenamed Mulberries and will be protected by Gooseberry blockships.

4 June 1944. 21.00 hours.   Below. The 'Most Secret' weather map of the North Atlantic which promises a respite of twenty-four hours between vigorous depressions and their associated south-westerly winds. It is 'chancy' and below 'minimum requirements,' explained the senior Overlord meteorologist, Group Captain J.N. Stagg, 'but it does represent something of a lull on Tuesday'. The Supreme Allied Commander, General Eisenhower, eventually made up his mind that Tuesday 6 June would be D-Day: "I am quite positive we must give the order... I don't like it, but there it is. I don't see how we can do anything else.'

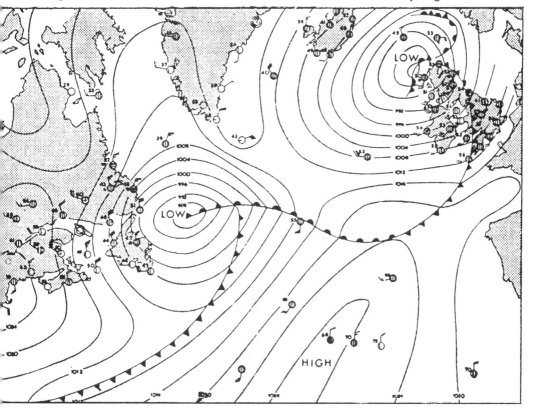

4 June 1944.
Dorchester. D-Day
briefing for an
American engineer
unit.
'The time has come
to deal the enemy a
terrific blow' –
Montgomery's
words were read to
all troops.
Prominent in the
foreground are
Private Albert V.
Ottolino of
Billings, Montana;
Private First-Class
Howard D. Kraut
of Brush,
Colorado; Private
J.H. James of
Woodville, Texas.

4-5 June 1944. Weymouth. Men of V
Corps (opposite, top) of the First
United States Army, with full kit
including rifles, pass out of the coffee
tent: 'From the folks back home
through the American Red Cross'.

1944. Weymouth. United States Military
Policeman Sergeant Daniel Ewton (left)
policed the town's invasion of GI s.

4-5 June 1944. Weymouth. Assault troops,
part of Force O tasked to storm Omaha Beach,
relaxing (opposite, below) with a quayside
dance on the eve of what they know is going to
be the worst day of their lives.

May 1944. Weymouth.
United States Army
Private Ernie Webster
and 20-year-old Regent
Cinema salesgirl Doris
Mockridge, of 12
Trinity Road. She sold
him a box of matches
and became a GI bride,
their romance being
movingly recounted by
John Murphy in his
'Dorset at War'. By the
time of the wedding,
back from Omaha
Beach, Ernie had lost a
leg.

4-5 June 1944. Weymouth Quay. Black 'static' troops of the United States Army load assault landing craft LCA 882 (the centre vessel in the pictures opposite).

4 June 1944. Farewell time, outside the Cove House Hotel as landlady Mrs Elizabeth Comben (centre) says goodbye to the United States Navy. Their individual stories are told by John Murphy in his 1979 book , 'Dorset at War'.

4-5 June 1944. Weymouth Quay and the old Ritz Theatre (burnt down in the 1950s and replaced by the Pavilion). Lines of Negro 'static' troops pass down stores to the American assault landing craft which are to lead Force O on to Omaha Beach in Normandy.

4-5 June 1944. Weymouth Quay. Opposite. Royal Navy ratings assist the embarkation of a Ranger battalion of V Corps of the United States Army, due to assault Omaha Beach at H-hour–06.45 hours on D-Day. They will hit the strongest resistance of the Normandy Landings, with Rangers being pinned down on the right on the right flank for several hours and suffering heavy casualties whilst their beachhead lay in the balance.

4-5 June 1944. Weymouth Harbour. Opposite the office of pleasure steamer operators Cosens and Co, landing craft prepare for departure. Lieutenant Robert T. Eldin (below, left) and First Lieutenant Stanley White looks suitably determined.

4-5 June 1944. Portland, opposite top, showing a line of American DUKWs beside the Chesil Beach, waiting their turn to go into landing craft at (above) and to join the armada that is being gathered (below) for the invasion of Normandy.

It is time for final briefings (opposite, centre) and the march of the American First Infantry Division southwards along Weymouth seafront (opposite, bottom) for embarkation at the Quay. Trucks were bound for the 'Hards' at Castletown, Portland (below).

1-5 June 1944. Portland and Weymouth. The 2nd Armored Division and V Corps of the United States Army, setting off for Omaha Beach and the invasion of Europe. In the pictures opposite, the tank landing craft are at Castletown Dockyard, Portland, and the infantry are filling on to smaller assault craft at Weymouth Quay. Everywhere in the two ports is a mass of men and equipment (below). For many of the GIs, June 6th would be the longest day of their lives. For the other thousand, however, it will be the shortest.

June 1944. Portland and Weymouth. The emblem that is everywhere around the two ports, and quite common at Poole as well: that of the 14th Major Port of the United States Army Transportation Corps.

4-5 June 1944.
Portland and Weymouth.
Above top, an American DUKW
reverses into a landing craft at
Castletown Docks, Portland. It goes in
backwards so that it can come out
forwards. Assault troops are packed
like sardines at Weymouth Quay
(above) and with trucks at Castletown
and Portland (overleaf). GIs break into
song (right) as they wait to board the
USS 'Henrico' at Weymouth.

5 June 1944. Portland Harbour. General Infantrymen of the United States Army aboard the troopship 'Henrico'. This should have been D-Day but turned into a day of standing around waiting when the weather caused the invasion to be postponed until the 6th.

4 June 1944. Portland Harbour. Material was almost as important as men. Supply launches were constantly speeding from the shore to the ships at anchor.

6 June 1944. Mid-Channel. Convoy in the Allied sea armada, protected by barrage balloons from air attacks that never came. Admiral Sir Bertram Ramsay, commanding the naval support for the greatest amphibious landings in history, described it as 'an air of unreality' because no U-boats were encountered and E-boats were kept in port by bad weather and the elimination of German radar stations. The remarkable series of photographs on this and the previous pages are from the Pentagon and courtesy of the United States Army.

5 June 1944. The British 6th Airborne Division prepares at Tarrant Rushton, Hurn, Holmsley South and other aerodromes to drop in tomorrow on Normandy. Above, the graffiti is defiant: 'The Channel stopped you, but not us. Remember Coventry, Plymouth, Bristol, London. Now its our turn. You've had your time you German ...' The original last word was rubbed out for the benefit of the photographer and eventual readers — but the men were allowed to have 'Swinhunds' instead.

Opposite. The men file towards lines of Horsa gliders painted with D-Day stripes, and a Tetrarch light tank is loaded into the belly of a Hamilcar. The Horsas were manufactured by Airspeed Limited at Christchurch.

5 June 1944. RAF Tarrant Rushton (above). Hamilcars and in particular number 770, preparing to lift
elements of the British 6th Airborne Division, RAF Hurn (opposite). The line-up
of Horsa troop carrying gliders and their Albemarle tug aircraft of 570 Squadron.

5 June 1944. Tarrant Rushton Aerodrome. British 6th Airborne Division prepares for D-Day.
Above. A Halifax tug-plane of 644 Squadron takes off with a Hamilcar glider.

Opposite, top. A Hamilcar (right) and Halifax combination over the Crichel Estate woodlands with Badbury
Rings (marked 'A') being just discernible. The planes have their D-Day stripes.
Opposite, below. A Hamilcar has its flaps down ready to land back at Tarrant Rushton. The skids on the
belly were to help if survive more difficult terrain.

Below. The Hamilcar (right) is towed by the Halifax over The Cliff escarpment and into the sky above
Tarrant Monkton.

A

5 June 1944. Tarrant Rushton Aerodrome, D-Day minus one: the Halifax tugs and their Horsa gliders (along the runway) prepare for a midnight date with history. The photograph is from the north and as on the last page the Iron Age hill-fort of Badbury Rings has been marked with an 'A'. The planes are on the east-west runway (actually east-north-east-west-south-west and the gliders are facing east-north-east; a south-westerly wind was still blowing but a lull was forecast, correctly).

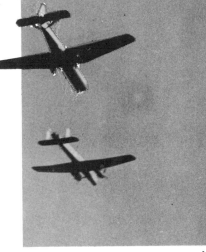

Opposite. The British 6th Airborne Division – airborne in a practice for the drop on Pegasus Bridge and the other vital crossing points near Caen. The tugs in this instance are RAF Whitley bombers.

6-7 June 1944. Pegasus Bridge. Hamilcars (opposite, top) and Horsa gliders from Tarrant Rushton (opposite) in the fields of Normandy. The latter craft detached their fuselages to disgorge men and equipment instantly. Major John Howard (top left) arrived with the 2nd Battalion, the Oxfordshire and Buckinghamshire Light Infantry, to capture Pegasus Bridge over the Caen Canal (above) and the nearby Horsa Bridge. His glider-borne troops were not reinforced by paratroops until three hours later, and 'then only in dribs and drabs' by 150 men out of a total of 500 who had been scattered widely across the surrounding countryside. The bridges are crucial to the holding of the Normandy beach-heads because any German offensive will have to come along this road which lies between Bénouville and Ranville, about three miles from the coast.

6 June 1944. Omaha Beach, offshore, inshore and on the shore. Assault landing craft plough towards Normandy, passing the flagship of Force O, United States Ship 'Augusta'. GIs wade ashore between bursts of withering enemy fire. Many are hit. One wounded infantryman is comforted by a comrade who removes his bandoleer. A third soldier turns his anguish towards the cameraman.

6 June 1944. Omaha Beach, at dawn. Above:
In deep water. Weymouth's Americans of the First Infantry Division, initially up to their
shoulders in the sea as they leap from an Assault Landing Craft. They are part of the first wave of
invaders, approaching a section of Omaha Beach and a line of low hills that are held by
determined German defenders.

6 June 1944. Omaha Beach, mid-afternoon. Right:
Consolidation. Back-up troops pile out from an Assault Landing Craft as Normandy's worst
landing zone is turned from a killing field into a beach head. Already ashore are DUKWs and
half-trucks, with the latter towing 57-mm anti-tank guns. Lines of GIs march towards the smoke,
where the front-line of German bunkers and batteries have now been battered into submission.

BEACH AND UNDERWATER OBSTACLES (Küstenvorfeldsperre)

Symbol	German	English
⊗	Holzpfähle seewärts geneigt mit eine T-Mine	Wooden stake slanting seawards with one T-Mine
	Hembalken seewärts geneigt mit Stahlmessern	Ramp slanting seawards with steel knives
	Hem balken mit Mine	Ramp with mine
✕	Tschechenigel auf Pfähle oder Betonsockel gesetzt	Hedgehog on stakes or on concrete base
⦀	Belgische Rollböcke, in weichen Boden auf Pfähle gesetzt, mit or ohne Mine	Element C (on soft ground supported by stakes) with or without mine
	Beton Tetraeder (O.T.) mit Stahlstachel	Concrete tetrahedra with steel stakes
	Tetraeder mit Mine	Tetrahedra with mine
	Betonhembalken (O.T.) Stahlmessern	Concrete ramp with steel knives
	Betonhembalken mit Mine	Concrete ramp with mine
	chwimmende Balkenmine	Floating raft with mine

6 June 1944. Warning signs. German military symbols, on a sheet issued to American GIs landing on Omaha Beach, so they can interpret the markings on any captured charts. In theory these 'Beach and Underwater Obstacles' should have been eliminated by aerial and naval bombardment. In fact, however, most remain intact. This document was produced by the Military Intelligence Research Section of the United States Army.

6 June 1944.
Omaha Beach.
Wreckage of
American
vehicles (right)
with a Sherman
tank knocked-out
beside the sand
dunes. From
here the German
defenders, of the
352nd Infanterie
Division, (below)
were pinning
down the
American 1st
Infantry
Division. In the
foreground is a
stick-grenada
and a Russian-
made 7.62-mm
machine-gun.
One of the GI
deaths at the first
hurdle (far right)
lies beside a
wooden stake,
above a
waterproof
Teller mine.

6 June 1944. British beachhead. Cromwell and Sherman tanks climb inland from the King (Red) sector of Gold Beach at La Rivière.

6 June 1944. British beachhead. The invasion of Normandy gathers pace as the tide recedes.

March/June 1944. Poole Bay test for Pluto, and the end result–the Pipe Line Under The Ocean Pumping petroleum into a beached tanker on the sands of Normandy.

13 June 1944. Destroyer HMS 'Boadicea' is sunk off Portland as the Germans counter-attack picks away at cross-channel supply convoys.

6 June and 12 August 1944. Portland Harbour. The 34,000-ton battleship HMS 'Rodney' sailed to bombard the Normandy beaches on D-Day and crossed the English Channel again in August, to pound German gun emplacements on Alderney in the Channel Islands.

19-22 June 1944. Mulberry Harbours, Normandy. Gales rocked the pontoon roads (above) and littered the beach with wreckage. The storms, described by General Montgomery as being 'of unprecedented violence,' disrupted the landing of ammunition and stores. It nearly destroyed the harbours, off the beaches of Arromanches, in the British sector, and near Vierville, in the American sector. The concrete caissons, codenamed Phoenix, began to arrive on D+3 (9 June) and are protected by an outer line of blockships, which in normal times hold back the waves (as in the photograph opposite). Pontoon causeways run from caissons to the shore (below and opposite).

5 June Hurn joins attacks on German radar stations.

Group Captain Denys Gillam, commanding 20 Sector at Thorney Island, with 22 Sector, under Group Captain Davoud at Hurn, have been responsible for the pre-D-Day attacks by the Allied Expeditionary Air Force on German radar stations in the English Channel.

Sir Trafford Leigh-Mallory, commanding AEAF, reported: "These radar targets were very heavily defended by flak, and low-level attacks upon them demanded great skill and daring. Losses among senior and more experienced pilots are heavy."

By the night of 5 June, fewer than ten of the forty-seven German radars were still able to transmit, and some of these have been deliberately preserved from Allied attack in order that they should relay bogus signals indicating an offensive in the area of the Pas-de-Calais.

5 June Hurn Wing Commander plucked from sea and back in air.

Reg Jones, the chief of scientific intelligence at the Air Ministry, writes in his *Most Secret War* that today he flew over the Solent and realised the invasion was 'on' because the armada that had been in Spithead two days before was no longer there.

He flew on to Hurn: "I was silently wishing them good luck when we had a head-on encounter with a whole wing of American Thunderbolts. It was like standing in a butt whilst a covey of enormous grouse is driven past you on all sides. What was more, the Thunderbolts with their big radial engines were climbing, and so none of their pilots could see us.

"We duly landed at Hurn, my main memory being of a Norwegian Wing Commander who had been taking part in the radar strikes. He had been shot down earlier that day, picked up out of the sea by one of the air-sea rescue launches, and had already flown another sortie."

Twenty-eight Typhoons had delivered ninety-six 60-lb rockets and seven tons of bombs on German coastal radar stations-taking care to keep that at Fecamp intact so that it could report spoof activity aimed at convincing the enemy that the main thrust of the Allied invasion is further up-Channel, east of the Seine.

Five squadrons of Typhoons and Mosquitoes are now operating from RAF Hurn, as are P-61 Black Widow night-fighters of the 9th United States Army Air Force and B-26 Marauders of the American 97th Bombardment Group.

5 June Battleship 'Rodney' in Weymouth Bay.

Weymouth Bay has its largest gathering of big warships since the Reserve Fleet was dispersed in 1939. The danger of air attack then prevented anything larger than a destroyer operating from Portland Harbour.

Operation Neptune has brought five American and two British cruisers to the bay, plus the strange cut-short silhouette of the 34,000-ton battleship HMS *Rodney*. The terrific destructive force of her broadsides is to be used tomorrow in French coastal bombardment – she is preparing to fire her full armament of nine 16-inch, twelve 6-inch and six 4.7-inch guns.

The great armada of smaller craft is to sail east up the English Channel, passing Bournemouth Bay, to gathering point Z to the south of the Isle of Wight. It will then turn due south for the assault crossing.

5 June   **Gliders ready at Tarrant Rushton.**

Painted with invasion-day stripes, trains of Horsa troop-carrying gliders are being prepared for take-off at Tarrant Rushton. The men are part of the British 6th Airborne Division and will drop to the east of the Normandy beachheads – at Benouville, Merville, Ranville, Varaville, Bures and Troarn – to hold the bridges on the River Orne and to break those across the River Dives.

In all thirty-nine aircraft are taking part from Tarrant Rushton Aerodrome. Six Halifax-Horsa combinations are involved in the surprise first wave attack, Operation Coup de Main. They are carrying a total of 171 troops and are under orders to capture intact the bridges across the Caen Canal and the River Orne to the north of Caen. After releasing the Horsa gliders these Halifax tow-craft will bomb a powder factory to the south-east of Caen to create a diversion.

Another thirty Halifax-Horsa combinations are detailed to carry out Operation Tonga. Their Horsa gliders will be released at point LZ-N, to the east of Caen Canal. The 3rd and 5th Parachute Brigades are involved in this drop, which is to begin about half-an-hour after Operation Coup de Main. Additionally a much smaller force, of only three Albemarle combinations, is tasked to take-out a German coast battery near Merville.

The first three gliders to leave Tarrant Rushton are being towed by twin-engined Albemarles and are those destined for the coast at Merville.

The following six gliders will be towed by four-engined Halifaxes and are also loaded with men from the Oxfordshire and Buckinghamshire Light Infantry, bound for the Orne swingbridge and canal bridge [to be known henceforth by the men's Pegasus emblem]. They are to leave shortly before midnight and are expected to be released about five miles short of their targets, at around 01.30 hours, to glide down on to French soil. Then the other thirty Halifax-Horsa combinations will take-off for Operation Tonga.

Once the infantry have secured the immediate dropping zones the two Halifax squadrons from Tarrant Rushton will return to France, at about 21.00 hours, in Operation Mallard, with a convoy of thirty gliders of the British 6th Air Landing Brigade – the larger Hamilcars with the Division's heavier equipment including Tetrarch tanks, Bren-gun carriers, twenty-five pounder field guns, scout cars and Bailey bridge pontoons.

The gliders are to be released over point LZ-N and eighteen containers are to be dropped at point DZ.

5 June   **Gliders lift off from Tarrant Rushton for 'Pegasus' bridge.**

22.56 hours. The first Halifax has roared along the central runway at

Tarrant Rushton Aerodrome and lifted off, towing a Horsa glider of the British 6th Airborne Division towards France. There are thirty-six Halifax tug-planes and their gliders to be cleared at one-minute intervals. 6th Airborne Division is commanded by 47-year-old Brigadier Richard Gale.

Into the sky has gone the 1st Platoon of 'D' Company of the 2nd Battalion, Oxfordshire and Buckinghamshire Light Infantry. They are commanded by Major John Howard.

He arrived with his men at Tarrant Rushton on 26 May and they have been confined to camp, awaiting the codeword to 'go' which arrived at 09.00 hours on Friday 4 June. To everyone's disappointment this was cancelled because of the windy weather.

This morning Major Howard received the order again and it has been another day of loading and re-checking, leading up to a fat-less evening meal to calm the men's stomachs, at this moment when everyone's faith is in the renowned abilities of the Glider Pilot Regiment. Faces are blackened and all have clambered aboard – for a promised gap in the German flak at Cabourg.

Howards 'D' Company will be cast off at 5,000 feet to land beside the bridge over the Caen Canal which is to be codenamed 'Pegasus' from the division's graphic shoulder-flash.

Footnote Operation Coup de Main – the surprise attack – proceeded smoothly with this section of 6th Airborne dropped near Benouville as planned and four of the six gliders only yards from their target spot. They were the first Allied soldiers to arrive in France on D-Day and opened the Second Front in the European theatre of war. Both bridges were secured intact.

"Ham and Jam, Ham and Jam," Lance-Corporal Edward Tappenden radioed from a captured pillbox fifteen minutes after the attack on 'Pegasus' bridge. It confirmed that D-Day's first battle had been successfully concluded.

Operation Tonga encountered more problems. Five of the aircraft failed to release their gliders within the landing zone and Halifax K288 went down with its port wing blazing.

A total of 670 Horsa gliders for the Airborne Divisions were constructed at the Airspeed factory beside Christchurch Aerodrome.

6 June   **Invasion Day – the sky fills.**

00.15 hours. Victor Swatridge of Dorchester Police was patrolling the town's Victoria Park with the intention of meeting his beat constable there at 00.30 hours. In 1971, Swatridge recalled what happened; he was witnessing the greatest mass movement of aircraft that has ever taken place:

"Britain was still suffering from its black-out and not a glimmer of light dared emit from any house or premises. It was a beautiful clear starlit night, when suddenly I became aware of the heavy drone of aircraft coming from inland. As it drew nearer, the sky lit up: thousands of coloured lights had burst forth and the whole atmosphere exploded into activity."

"It was an amazing transformation as hundreds of bombers towing gliders with their masses of human and vehicle cargo flew overhead and across the English Channel. This huge armada was a continuous procession for more than two hours. It was clearly evident that the invasion of Europe had commenced and I remember how excited I was. But yet the civilian population were still quietly sleeping in their beds; everyone had become immune to the noise of aircraft travelling overhead, yet I venture to suggest if it had been enemy planes, the whole place would have been alive with activity, sirens would have wailed and woken them from their slumber."

"Invasion Day had been very secretively guarded; everyone had been warned that it would be treasonable to give the slightest indication to the enemy that it was about to take place, and the civil population kept that bargain. The police had been warned to expect heavy counter bombing and we were expecting frightening reprisals. We waited but no enemy air action occurred to our utter amazement."

6 June **Weymouth wakes up to sound of the air armada.**

Twenty-two-year-old Weymouth teacher Miss Barbara Baker writes in her diary: "Early this morning was awakened by the throbbing of low-flying aircraft. Looked out of the window and saw the sky full of bombers towing gliders. Presume airborne troops are being dropped behind enemy lines in France? Heard later that all ships anchored in Weymouth Bay had sailed across the Channel to land troops in Normandy. The long awaited invasion has begun."

The first day back at school after the Whitsun holiday was already on its way into history.

6 June **D-Day.**

The sea forces deployed today, Tuesday, are an armada unequalled in history – 138 warships carrying out bombardments; 221 destroyers and other escort vessels; 287 minesweepers; 491 miscellaneous light craft; 441 auxiliaries-quite apart from the more than 4,000 landing craft that they are supporting and protecting. Merchant vessels are also involved in a myriad of support roles, to a total of 6.488 vessels acting under Admiralty instructions.

6 June **'Fishpond' reveals the Dorset armada.**

The armada off Dorset of V Corps of the First United States Army on their way from Weymouth and Portland towards Omaha Beach was such a concentration of steel that it showed on the Fishpond airborne radar set in Roland Hammersley's aircraft.

His first report of the blips sent the pilot, Ron Walker, looking for an enemy fighter force, but they saw to their astonishment the flotillas of landing craft heading towards Normandy. What Roland does not realise is that his brother, Walter, is down there on the sea.

Roland Hammersley was born at Swanage and lives at Bovington. He is a gunner with 57 Squadron, and took off this morning at 01.36 hours in a Lancaster bomber from East Kirkby, Lincolnshire, on a mission to attack coastal gun emplacements at La Pernelle.

6 June **Dorset's Americans get the bloodiest beach.**

H-hour for Dorset's American, when they were to begin the assault on Omaha beach, was set at 06.45 hours this morning. In the event, 06.34 was the moment the first troops touched the sands of Normandy, but that was about all that went ahead of schedule for V Corps of the 1st United States Army.

They attacked on a broad front – ten miles wide – with two regimental combat teams, one each from the 29th Infantry Division and the 1st Infantry Division, supplemented by Ranger Battalions. The 29th Division is tasked to capture Vierville-sur-Mer as its initial target, while the 1st Division is to secure Colleville-sur-Mer, about three miles to the east. The landing beaches for Force O extend from Pointe du Hoc to Colleville, to the north-west of Bayeux which is famous for an invasion tapestry depicting an assault on the other side of the Channel.

Heavy seas and numerous underwater obstacles have caused considerable losses to the leading wave of Americans in amphibious tanks and landing craft. Aerial bombing had been hampered by poor visibility and mostly fell some distance inland, added to which the naval bombardment was also largely ineffective, due to the topography of the ground.

Worse was to follow. It is now known that the German coastal forces were recently augmented by the 352nd Infanterie Division, a field formation which happened to be holding a stand-to exercise and was manning the defences as the Americans came ashore. They ran into an enemy division that was ready for action and were pinned to the beaches. Likewise the Ranger Battalions on the right flank met with stiff resistance and V Corps have undoubtedly received the bloodiest reception of the day.

For several hours it has seemed that they might well be thrown back into the sea. Extreme sacrifice and gallantry – leaving a thousand dead and twice that number wounded – has by nightfall achieved a beachhead a mile in depth, between Vierville and Colleville. This foothold was established after follow-up regimental terms had arrived. These reinforcements enabled the storming of the enemy batteries. Forward elements are now two miles inland, pushing towards higher ground in the vicinity of Formigny.

The novelist Ernest Hemingway has arrived as a war correspondent with the assault forces aboard the troopship *Dorothea L. Dix*, from Portland.

Major Stanley Bach, the liaison officer giving General Cota's orders to the 1st Division assault troops on the beach, scrawled these potted descriptions of the day on a couple of old envelopes which were his only available paper.

"11.30. Mortar, rifle, 88-mm and machine gun fire so heavy on beach, it's either get to ridge in back of beach or be killed."

"Noon. Beach high tide, bodies floating. Many dead Americans on beach at high-water mark."

"12.15. Heavy mortar and 88-mm fire started on beach from east end to west end – series of five shells in spots. Direct hit on Sherman tank, men out like rats – those alive."

"12.30. LCT [tanking landing craft] hit two mines, came on in – hit third, disintegrated and rear end sank. At burst of shell two Navy men went flying through the air into water and never came up."

"14.40. More mortar fire and more men hit. LCVP [personnel landing craft] unload five loads of men, they lie down on beach, mortar fire kills five of them, rest up and run to fox holes we left a couple of hours ago."

"16.50. Established CP [command post] and saw first time the 1st Division friends who were quiet, fighting men – gave me heart."

"17.00. Prisoners began to come up road – a sorry looking bunch in comparison to our well-fed and equipped men."

"Dusk. I've seen movies, assault training demonstrations and actual battle but nothing can approach the scenes on the beach from 11.30 to 14.00 hours – men being killed like flies from unseen gun positions. Navy can't hit 'em, air cover can't see 'em – so infantry had to dig 'em out."

Footnote The Americans could indeed have lost the beach if German High Command had not held back their reserve units, thinking that the Normandy assaults were a feint and that the main invasion force would land between the Seine and Calais. Overlord fielded a total of 39 divisions but the Germans wildly exaggerated its strength, believing that between 75 and 85 divisions had been assembled for the Allied second front; this belief caused them to hold back their forces in preparation for the non-existent second half.

6 June   **1st Dorsets among first Britons ashore in France.**

Army Operation Overlord/ Navy Operation Neptune/ Air Force Operation Mallard. Supported by the cruiser HMS *Emerald* and the destroyers HMS *Cottesmore, Grenville, Jervis, Ulysses, Undine* and *Urania*, with the Polish destroyer *Krakowiak*, plus the softening-up efforts of four fighter-bomber squadrons, the 1st Battalion of the Dorsetshire Regiment left LCH317 and touched down on the beach to the north-east of the village of Les Roquettes at 07.30 hours. 'A' Company is led by Major A.A.E. Jones and 'B' Company by Major P. Chilton.

They have landed in the Jig (Green) sector of the Gold Beach bridgehead and with the Hampshires – a thousand yards to the east-can claim to be the first British troops to land in Normandy from the sea.

Captain C.R. Whittington, the Unit Landing Officer, wore a rainbow-coloured battle bowler. He was soon wounded but continued organising the clearing of corridors up the beach. Major Jones was withdrawn wounded and Major Chilton led the crossing of the minefields.

'C' Company [Major R.M. Nicholl] and 'D' Company [Major W.N. Hayes], helped the Hampshires take Asnelles-sur-Mer and proceeded to attack high ground at Point 54. 'C' Company had most of the fighting though the enemy eventually abandoned its four 155-mm guns and by

18.00 the 1st Dorsets had found convenient dugouts for Battalion Headquarters on the hillside north of Ryes.

'B' Company moved into Ryes, which had been captured by the Devons.

The Dorsets have achieved all the day's objectives but at the cost of heavy losses – three officers killed; thirty other ranks killed; eleven officers wounded; eighty-four other ranks wounded.

6 June   Hurn Typhoons notch up 88 sorties.

Air Operation Mallard, the RAF's contribution to Operation Overlord, has been sweeping across the Normandy beachheads all day.

The Typhoons of 83 Group of the 2nd British Tactical Air Force have flown eighty-eight cross-Channel sorties from RAF Hurn today in ground support attacks on enemy positions and the railway lines along which their reinforcements would come.

6 June   Warmwell sorties over the Cherbourg peninsula.

Today and for the next nine days the American Lightnings of the 474th Fighter Group from Warmwell will dive-bomb strategic targets in the Cherbourg peninsula and cover convoys of Allied shipping.

Footnote The Americans lost two pilots on these combat air patrols, Lieutenant Doty and Lieutenant Robert Hanson. A second Robert Hanson also flew with the 474th and survived to organise an association of its ex-members.

6 June   HMS 'Lyme Regis' clears Monty's passage.

The minesweeper HMS *Lyme Regis*, paid for and adopted by the west Dorset town in 1941-42, is clearing a safe channel into Sword Beach at the eastern end of the Normandy bridgehead. She is buoying it with French tricolour pennants.

The swept channel is being prepared for the passage into France of General Sir Bernard Montgomery and the Advance Headquarters staff of 21st Army Group.

7 June Hurn Typhoons fly 138 Normandy sorties.

As the front lines widen in Normandy so the air-war intensifies. Typhoons of 83 Group of the 2nd British Tactical Air Force have been taking off and landing at RAF Hurn all day.

They have logged 138 sorties in support of the Second British Army on the coast north of Caen.

There are many Canadian flyers operating from Hurn and their special interest is with the central beachhead – the Juno sector – where the 3rd Canadian Infantry Division and the 2nd Canadian Armoured Brigade went ashore at Courseulles.

8 June   Surviving rocket-firing craft limp into Poole.

The first of the returnee vessels from the Normandy landings are a group of LCRs, American rocket-firing landing craft, which have limped into Poole Harbour peppered with shell-holes after their onslaught against the enemy beaches.

10 June   Hurn Typhoons manage a record 154 Normandy sorties.

The Typhoons of 83 Group of the 2nd British Tactical Air Force have had a record day. They went on 154 sorties from RAF Hurn.

Pilot Officer Grey of 181 Squadron has become the first Hurn fighter pilot to stand upon liberated Europe.

He found himself in difficulties and brought his Typhoon down on to a newly-made temporary airstrip. Later he was able to return to Hurn with the story.

13 June HMS 'Boadicea' sinks off Portland.

HMS *Boadicea*, a Royal Navy destroyer, has been sunk off Portland with the loss of almost all her crew. She was a mile or so ahead of convoy EBC8, steaming up-Channel at 6 knots, and was herself zig-zagging at 9 knots when what was thought to be an allied aircraft approached at 04.45 hours this morning. RAF Beaufighters had been seen in the area.

Instead, descending towards her port side, it was a Junkers Ju188 bomber and in the process of releasing two aerial torpedoes. The second hit *Boadicea's* forward magazine and the resultant explosion instantaneously destroyed the front half of the ship. The stern half was immediately inundated and sank in a couple of minutes.

There were only a dozen survivors, picked-up by the destroyer HMS *Vanquisher* and taken to Portland.

13 June   More ships lost by both sides.

The past three days have seen other sinkings off the Dorset coast, as the German 2nd Schnellboot Flotilla evacuated Cherbourg and regrouped in Ostend from where it is concentrating on the supply convoys.

As Supply Convoy S-NS 08 assembled in Poole Bay it was seen by a German reconnaissance plane and intercepted by the Schnellboote in mid-Channel. S177 sank the *Brackenfield*, a 657-ton steamer, and the *Ashanti*, 534 tons. S178 claimed the *Dungrange*, 621 tons. A Norwegian destroyer, the *Stord*, sailed to the aid of the convoy with units of the Royal Navy but the Schnellboote outpaced them and escaped to Boulogne.

Some German losses have been sustained by the E-boat force in the past three days, however, as RAF Beaufighters of 143 Squadron and 236 Squadron, operating from the New Forest, have claimed to have damaged or sunk three Schnellboote, one Raumboot mine-layer, plus a Minensuchboot, minesweeper. Two of the fighters failed to return; one being brought down by anti-aircraft fire and the other credited to a Messerschmitt Me163 Komet rocket-propelled fighter.

Footnote John Pitfield tells me that a Komet could not have brought down the Beaufighter as these German rocket-propelled planes had a short range and were operational only from German airfields. He says that it was a mistaken identification of one of the other remarkable new planes which the Germans deployed as the war drew to a close, either a Messerschmitt 262 or an Arado 234C, with the former being most likely. These jets had top speeds of 541 mph and 530 mph respectively. The poor Beaufighter could only do 320 mph.

13 June   **500-lb bomb removed from Highcliffe.**

11.50 hours. A 500-lb bomb that fell at Woolhayes, Highcliffe, on 15 May has been removed by a bomb disposal unit.

14 June **Bomber Command soups up defence of the Channel.**

Bomber Command has supplied some four-engine aircraft to 19 Group, RAF Coastal Command, who are now hard-pressed to keep the English Channel reasonably safe for the convoys supplying the Normandy forces.

Footnote By the end of June, No.19 Group had sunk fourteen German U-boats in the Channel, three of them in the Dorset sector between Start Point and the Isle of Wight.

15 June   **Portland divers carry out underwater welding.**

To the surprise of American engineer James Spearman and the rest of the unit in LCT 1000, major seam repairs to its bottom have been carried out underwater in Portland Harbour. The tank landing craft turned back for England after cracking across the middle in rough seas.
She carries a Bailey bridge-building outfit, trucks and pontoons.

Footnote LCT 1000 was by no means the only casualty of the storm. Unfavourable weather during the first five days after D-Day meant that only thirty-eight percent of the planned tonnage of stores was actually brought ashore on the American sectors.

16 June   **U-boat sinks HMS 'Blackwood' off Portland.**

Last night the 3rd Escort Group of the Royal Navy, steaming at 12 knots off Portland, lost the frigate HMS *Blackwood* to a torpedo from U-764.
   The mast instantly disappeared and the bridge folded backwards in a tremendous explosion of yellow smoke at 19.11 hours. It left the bows and stern raised almost out of the water.
   RAF-Air Sea Rescue launches HSL 2696 and 2697 were joined by the frigate HMS *Essington* as the crew abandoned ship. By about 21.00 hours all were taken off. Of the survivors about thirty-five are wounded.
   The wreck remained afloat almost until dawn, with radar contact being lost at 04.10 hours this morning.

16 June   **An American bombs Warmwell.**

As an engine cut-out on his aircraft at Warmwell, American pilot Lieutenant Cumbie of the 430th Squadron followed standard procedure and jettisoned his bombs, which – contrary to correct procedure – turned out to be armed. He scored a direct hit on the field's transformer station.

The pilot returned safely to the airfield, to congratulations from its RAF contingent: "Jerry's been trying to hit that for years!"

18 June   **Supply ship sunk.**

A supply ship, the 1,764-ton *Albert C. Field*, has been sunk by German aircraft off Dorset. She was heading from south Wales to the Normandy beaches. Her owners are the Upper Lakes and St Lawrence Transportation Company.

21 June   **War interrupts Warmwell's dress parade.**

The American pilots of the 474th Fighter Group, dressed for inspection by General Kincaid at Warmwell when they were to receive medals, instead received an unexpected order to scramble and found themselves back over France.

Two of the Lightnings were lost, killing Lieutenant Vinson. The other pilot, Captain Larson, parachuted to safety and lived to receive the medal.

Footnote Three other Warmwell pilots, Lieutenants Gee, Heuermann and Danish were killed in the last week of June as the Americans harried the railway system in northern France. Many of the attacks were on targets of opportunity."You guys can just go over and hit anything that moves," they had been told.

22 June   **Airborne rescue turns into a boat trip.**

Lieutenant Dumar of 509 Squadron of the 405th Fighter Bomber Group of the United States Army Air Force, flying a Thunderbolt from Christchurch, had three lucky escapes today off the enemy coast.

His engine seized over the German side of the English Channel, thirty miles from Cherbourg, and he parachuted into the sea.

He was located and picked up by a Walrus amphibian of the Air-Sea Rescue service. Then the Walrus found itself in difficulties as the choppy conditions prevented it from lifting off.

The crew decided to taxi through the waves and make for home on the surface. The Walrus was nothing more nor less than a sitting duck for the forty-mile slog back into home waters but fortunately no one from the Luftwaffe happened along.

23 June   **Hurn Mosquitoes claim six Ju88s over Normandy.**

The night prowl of the Hurn Mosquitoes took in the Normandy beachheads last night and the pilots returned with claims of six kills. They had intercepted a formation of Junkers Ju88 bombers.

Squadron-Leader Petrie claimed two and Flying Officer Grey three, for 125 Squadron, and Flight-Lieutenant Sandemann claimed one for 604 Squadron.

The gale which has raged across the Channel for three days finally eased last night.

23 June   **US 3rd Armored Division embarked from Weymouth.**

The 3rd Armored Division of the United States Army is now landing on Omaha White Beach, near Isigny, for the tank actions that will decide the Battle of Normandy. The craft had been kept in Portland Harbour for the past four days by a violent gale. Others have crossed from Southampton Water.

The arrivals include the 32nd and 33rd Armored Regiments, supported by the 486th Armored Anti-Aircraft Battalion and the 23rd Armored Engineer Battalion. Headquarters staff and the division's artillery, the 54th, 67th and 391st Armored Field Artillery Battalions, are following tomorrow.

Footnote The 36th Armored Infantry Regiment arrived on the 25th.

24 June   **Bridport officer killed in Normandy.**

Lieutenant-Colonel J.W. Atherton, from Bridport, was killed today in Normandy. He was blown up by a shell whilst fighting off a counter-attack by German tanks. Until recently Colonel Atherton was with the 5th Battalion of the Dorsetshire Regiment.

25 June   **Two U-boats sunk off Portland.**

In the past twenty-four hours two German U-boats have been destroyed between Portland Bill and Start Point by patrol ships of the Royal Navy's invasion-landing escort groups that have been shadowing the constant Normandy shuttle-service that has continued all month.

Last night the frigates HMS *Affleck* and *Balfour* accounted for U-1191. Today it was the turn of HMS *Bickerton* to sink U-269. The frigate then left her group to pick up survivors and take them into port.

Meanwhile another frigate, HMS *Goodson,* was hit in the stern by an acoustic torpedo from U-984. Though crippled she is still floating and has been towed from mid-Channel to the coaling wharf at Portland. There are many casualties and the damage is irreparable.

25 June   **Portland Task Force bombards Cherbourg.**

Commanded by Rear Admiral Deyo, a formidable Task Force departed from Portland at 04.30 hours this morning, to bombard the German gun emplacements that defend the port of Cherbourg. Its capture is seen as vital to the next stage of Battle of Normandy.

Split into two bombardment groups, the fleet comprises three battleships – United States Ships *Texas*, *Arkansas* and *Nevada* – and four cruisers. These are the USS *Tuscaloosa* and *Quincy*, with HMS *Glasgow* and HMS *Enterprise*. They are protected by nine destroyer escorts.

Two hundred rounds were pounded into German batteries to the east and west of the port but some of the return fire was accurate. *Glasgow* was hit twice and there were injuries on the bridge of *Enterprise* from shell fragments. She has headed to Portsmouth.

The other ships returned to Portland by 19.30 this evening and a bomb disposal team have been called to Admiral Deyo's flagship, *Texas*. They are removing an unexploded 240-mm shell that penetrated the warrant officers' bunks.

Meanwhile advance units of General Joe Collins's VII Corps of the United States Army broke into Cherbourg, capturing two of the main forts and reaching the arsenal.

26 June St Alban's Head battle sends Germans packing.

Last night there was short but fierce naval engagement off St Alban's Head which resulted in German Schnellboote S130 and S168 departing for Dieppe, and S145 sustaining damage and being forced to flee for repairs to the nearest bastion that the enemy still holds; the occupied Channel Island of Alderney.

26 June   Change-over of Typhoons at Hurn.

With the gathering momentum of the siege of Cherbourg, following the capture of its Maupertus airfield on 23 June, the Typhoons of 124 and 143 Wings from RAF Hurn are now stationed in Normandy.

They comprise 83 Group of the 2nd British Tactical Air Force and are being replaced at Hurn by the arrival of 123 and 136 Wings, also with Typhoons.

These, together with 146 Wing which is also coming to Hurn, comprise 84 Group of the Second British Tactical Air Force.

29 June   Sixteen killed as Thunderbolts crash on Mudeford.

Foxwood Avenue at Mudeford, Christchurch, was devastated today by three American P-47 Thunderbolt fighter-bombers in two separate mishaps on take-off from Christchurch Advance Landing Ground. In the first, at 06.45 hours, the pilot survived and no one was hurt on the ground.

Then at 14.00 hours the same pilot tried again to take off. Once more he failed to gain proper height and overshot the runway into a bungalow. His fuel tanks and bombs exploded, bringing down another Thunderbolt, Scarab 2, that was coming off the runway. It was thrown upside down but the pilot, Lieutenant Drummond, escaped unhurt. The three planes belonged to the 509th Squadron of the 405th Fighter Bomber Group of the United States Army Air Force.

As rescue workers pulled the wounded out of the debris another bomb exploded, killing a fireman and wounding others. Sixteen are dead and eighteen injured.

The mortally wounded pilot, 22-year-old Lieutenant Vincent R. James, was comforted by nurse Irene Stevenson. He died in her arms in Boscombe Hospital.

Footnote Mrs Stevenson would become a local councillor and Mayor of Christchurch. Lieutenant James, who was unmarried, is buried at Cambridge American Cemetery. The 405th Fighter Bomber Group, based at Christchurch, lost a total of fifteen pilots during June 1944.

29 June Hurn Mosquitoes show the Yanks how to do it in the dark.

The Mosquito pilots of 125 Squadron at RAF Hurn are showing the twelve crewmen of six P-61 Black Widow night-fighters of the 71st Fighter Wing of the 9th United States Army Air Force how to carry out blind radar-guided interceptions.

The Black Widows flew in today from Charmy Down, near Bath, and will be taken up on operational night interception flights.

Footnote The Americans left on 10 July.

1 July Wessex forces the Odon bridgehead.

The Infantry of the 43rd (Wessex) Division have been fighting alongside the 15th (Scottish) Division since 28 June to force through the advance on the Odon bridgehead, against fierce Panzer counter-attacks.

2 July Another Thunderbolt crashes at Christchurch.

Today at 17.00 hours, an American P-47 Thunderbolt landed short of Christchurch Aerodrome and came down in a perimeter field. It bounced on to the adjacent Lymington road and fell to rest upside down. There was no fire and the pilot escaped.

3 July Twelve Tarrant Rushton aircraft in SOE operation.

Twelve aircraft from Tarrant Rushton Aerodrome are tonight tasked to fly over occupied France for the Special Operations Executive. Men and materials will be dropped to the Resistance. Four Halifax aircraft are being provided by 298 Squadron and four from 644 Squadron.

Additionally the station has on stand-by the four aircraft that have been used on a regular basis for such operations, two Stirlings from 299 Squadron and two from 196 Squadron.

5 July Christchurch Yanks give a Brit a Thunderbolt.

The Yanks lent a Brit a plane for the day, sent him out on a combat sortie over enemy occupied France, and then had kittens when he failed to return. Lieutenant Harris of the Royal Navy's Fleet Air Arm, a glider-tug pilot seconded to Airspeed Limited at Christchurch which makes Horsa troop-carriers, had talked 511 Squadron of the 405th Fighter Bomber Group of the United States Army Air Force into loaning him a Thunderbolt. He joined Blue Flight which today lifted off from Station 416, the Advance Landing Ground that is Christchurch Aerodrome, and crossed the English Channel. They beat up the railway system southwards across Brittany to Nantes.

The pilots of 511 Squadron returned to Christchurch for a de-briefing on their targets of opportunity and the bombing of a tunnel. Their fears grew as their British friend failed to join them – the concern was not just for him but that a court martial would result from the unauthorised loan and loss of the aircraft. Several hours later the panic turned to relief as Lieutenant Harris came home. He had overstayed his flying time in Brittany and had to force-land on an Allied-occupied beach in Normandy. Soldiers found him the petrol to take-off for a nearby captured airfield, where he was refuelled for the return flight to Christchurch.

6 July   Christchurch Thunderbolts trap train in tunnel.

A train driver in Lisieux in German-occupied France, on the eastern side of the Allied front-line, today took refuge in a tunnel as United States Army Air Force fighter-bombers attacked. His train was safe but their bombs left it trapped.

Thunderbolts of the 405th Fighter Bomber Group, which had flown across the Channel from Christchurch, scored direct hits at each end of the tunnel.

Improved weather is enabling concentrated air support to be provided for our troops. Lancasters and Halifaxes of Bomber Command are being prepared for attacks on German tanks and strong-points north of Caen, and against rocket-related structures in the Pas de Calais.

6 July   Warmwell's two-all air battle over Brittany.

Clear weather saw Warmwell's American P-38 Lightning fighter-bombers streaking across north-west France once again but today they met with a flight of more than twenty Focke-Wulf 190s.

Though they were able to claim two definite kills the Americans returned across the Channel without Lieutenants Rubal and Jacobs.

Footnote In another bombing run over France, against the rail network, Lieutenant Moore was killed when his plane ploughed into a bridge.

9 July   Pigeon post from Normandy to Hurn in seven hours.

Pigeons supplied from Bournemouth lofts have been arriving at RAF Hurn today some seven hours after release from the battle grounds in Normandy.

They are helping the front-line troops to keep contact with their air support units; in fact they are proving themselves as an air support unit.

11 July 1944. The 1st Battalion of the Dorsetshire Regiment fighting in Normandy. Sergeant Turner and Privates Martin, Torrington (a Canadian 'Dorset'), and Smith, with Lance-Corporal Wiltshire, are firing a three-inch mortar near Hottot. In the picture below the infantry and antitank guns are advancing along a tank track that has smashed through the hedgerows of the Bocage.

10 July   Hurn's 604 Squadron claims its hundredth kill.

The Mosquito night fighters of 604 Squadron at RAF Hurn have claimed their one hundredth kill.

Last night, Wing Commander Gerald Maxwell shot down a Junkers Ju88 and claimed a Dornier Do217 as a probable kill, which took the claims total to its century.

11 July   Thunderbolts leave Christchurch for Normandy.

The noise, excitement and danger from bomb-laden crash-landings have ended for the people of Christchurch as the Thunderbolts of the 405th Fighter Bomber Group take off from Station 416 for the last time. They are heading for Airstrip 8, at Picauville, in the Allied-occupied Cherbourg peninsula.

They have left Christchurch Aerodrome to the plane and glider makers Airspeed Limited, and an American flag to the Priory church as a memento of the United States Army Air Force. Their thousand-strong contingent will also leave a certain silence on the ground as the public houses and Bournemouth's places of entertainment clear up after the goodbyes to their liveliest clientele of all time.

14 July   Hurn Mosquitoes change-over.

The Mosquito night-fighters of 604 Squadron left RAF Hurn yesterday and were replaced today by Mark VI Mosquitoes flown in by the Canadians of 418 (City of Edmonton) Squadron.

They will work with 125 Squadron in Anti-Diver sorties against incoming Doodlebug flying bombs. The aim is to intercept and shoot down these V1 weapons over the sea eastwards of the Isle of Wight.

18 July   Warmwell Americans claim ten FW 190s.

The 474th Fighter Group from Warmwell routed a formation of twenty-five Focke-Wulf 190s over north-west France. They claimed ten, for the loss of three Lightnings.

Two of the Americans baled out but the third, Lieutenant Goodrich, died in his plane.

20 July   84 Group Typhoons leave Hurn for France.

The three Wings of 84 Group of the 2nd British Tactical Air Force, flying Typhoons from RAF Hurn, lifted off today to re-group in France.

23 July   Mosquito crashes at Poole.

A Mosquito fighter-bomber of 418 (City of Edmonton) Squadron, on low-level daylight flight over Poole, has crashed 200 yards west of Alder Road Drill Hall. It appears to have been pulling out of a roll when a wing struck the roof of a building in Mossley Avenue.

There was only slight damage to the house but the aircraft exploded shortly after hitting the ground. Both crewmen, Pilot Officers Bowhay and Naylor of the Royal Canadian Air Force, were killed.

27 July   Warmwell pilot killed over Tours.

Lieutenant Patton, flying a Lightning from Warmwell on a reconnaissance mission over Tours, was killed in an attack by a number of Messerschmitt Me109s.

July   Hurn Mosquitoes bomb the V-3.

Mosquitoes of 418 (City of Edmonton) Squadron and 125 (Newfoundland) Squadron, from Hurn, flew together in a bombing raid against the massive concrete emplacement of the German H.D.P. secret weapon project at Mimoyecques, near Calais. The Hochdruckpumpe [High Pressure Pump] is known to British scientific intelligence as the V-3 and is presumed to be a long-range gun.

Footnote Its intended function was not discovered until the site was overrun by the Second Canadian Corps in the last week of September 1944. Fifty smooth-bore barrels of 15 centimetres diameter, 127 metres in length, were pointed towards London and designed to fire finned projectiles, each weighing 300 lbs, at the rate of ten per minute. The technical achievement was a muzzle departure-velocity of 5,000 feet per second, reached by boosting the firing charges with further propellants in side ports along the barrels, but there had been a major hitch in the physics. Above speeds of 3,300 feet per second the shells toppled erratically. Even with more time and less bombing they would have fallen well short of the capital.

July   American Liberator crashes on Furzey Island.

An American Liberator bomber has crashed in Poole Harbour, hitting Furzey Island, with the loss of all its crew.

July   Wounded American pilots rest at Shaftesbury.

The American Red Cross are using Coombe House, near Shaftesbury, as a recuperation centre for wounded and exhausted bomber crews.

Footnote In 1945 the Institute of the Blessed Virgin Mary acquired the building and it became St Mary's Convent. The house stands in its own wooded valley, a few hundred yards across the county boundary, in the Wiltshire parish of Donhead St Mary.

1 August   Mosquito night-fighters quit Hurn.

The Mosquitoes of RAF Hurn were leaving today. Both 125 and 418

Squadrons are being redeployed at Middle Wallop, on the Hampshire Downs, though from there they can still venture into the night skies above Dorset in the unlikely event of German raiders coming this far west.

3 August **USAAF takes over RAF Hurn.**

The B-26 Marauders of 596, 597 and 598 Squadrons of the 97th Bombardment Croup of the 9th United States Army Air Force have taken over Hurn Aerodrome from the Royal Air Force.

3 August **Another Warmwell pilot dies in France.**

Lieutenant Chamberlain, flying an American Lightning fighter from Warmwell on a combat air patrol over France, has been killed by enemy action.

4 August **Sea-shell lands in Christchurch.**

A shell fell this afternoon in the garden of 36 Seafield Road, Christchurch. Fortunately it failed to explode. It had been fired from the sea, during gunnery practice by an unknown Allied vessel.

5 August **Warmwell's Americans move to French base.**

The 474th Fighter Group of the United States Army Air Force flew their final patrols from Warmwell today and landed on an airstrip in Normandy.

This advance base on the other side of the Channel has been used for the past five days for refuelling and is now the Group's temporary home for the next stage of the war in Europe. Two Messerschmitt Me 109s were claimed as kills on their moving day.

12 August **HMS 'Rodney' bombards Alderney.**

At 07.30 hours the battleship HMS *Rodney* steamed gracefully from Portland Harbour, escorted by the destroyers HMS *Jervis* and *Faulkner*, on a course that took them southwards into the Channel.

She was heading for the Channel Islands, where the battleship opened fire with her huge forward turrets of 16-inch guns on four German gun emplacements on the occupied island of Alderney. A total of seventy-five rounds were fired, hitting three of the batteries, in a bombardment that extended from 14.12 hours until 16.44.

The ships then made their way safely back to Portland, returning at 22.12.

14 August **Hurn Yanks blow-up German ammo train.**

B-26 Marauders of the American 97th Bombardment Group, flying from Hurn, have returned from a spectacular raid on the railway marshalling yards at Corbeil to the south of Paris.

They caught an ammunition train in the sidings. It was destined for the front-line troops of the German First Army.

18 August   RAF returns to Hurn for Air-Sea Rescue.

Three Walrus amphibians and six Air-Sea Rescue Spitfires of 277 Squadron have transferred from Warmwell Aerodrome to Hurn.

The American B-26 Marauders of the 97th Bombardment Group are due to leave Hurn for France in two days.

Footnote 277 Squadron went back to Warmwell on 29 August.

28 August   Wessex troops first across the Seine.

Eight separate battalion attacks were launched today by the 43rd (Wessex) Division to put the first British troops across the River Seine. Among them were the 5th Battalion of the Dorsetshire Regiment.

Footnote Lieutenant-General Brian Horrocks, the commander of 30th Corps, described it as "an epic operation". The logistical support behind the Allied advance had become stupendous and more than sufficient in everything except petrol. The Allies now had two million men and half a million vehicles in France. In tanks their numerical advantage over the Germans was twenty to one.

August   German Panzers to be tested at Lulworth.

Advanced examples of German armour – including Tiger and Panther tanks of the Panzer Lehr and other divisions of the retreating Panzer Group West – are being shipped to England for evaluation on the gunnery ranges of the Armoured Fighting Vehicles School at Lulworth Camp.

In excess of 650 German tanks and thousands of other vehicles were destroyed during the annihilation of German forces caught in the Falaise-Mortain pocket, the bottlenecked salient of the enemy front-line that was finally closed in the area of Chambois after limited escapes on 20 August. Often the Germans had immobilised themselves in bumper to bumper traffic congestion which provided Allied pilots with their easiest pickings of the war. The wreckage was on such a colossal scale that in places it brought the Allied advance to a halt.

German total losses are now in the order of 1,500 tanks and 3,500 guns destroyed or captured in the Battle of Normandy, plus tens of thousands of other vehicles from armoured car to horse and cart. The Wehrmacht has also lost nearly half a million men. The dead and wounded are estimated to number 240,000 and the number of Allied prisoners has reached 210,000.

Footnote The strategy for the Americans to break-out from the west of Normandy and pivot round towards the Seine, whilst the British and Canadians pinned down German armour east of Caen, was devised by

General Sir Bernard Montgomery. His promotion, to Field-Marshal, would be confirmed by King George VI on 1 September 1944.

August   **Poole blast kills three.**

Three naval ratings were killed and six hurt when ammunition detonated itself in one of the landing craft at HMS Turtle, the Royal Navy's shore-base at Poole. The vessel was destroyed and nearby buildings damaged.

17 September   **Tarrant Rushton Hamilcars join Arnhem airlift.**

Nearly a hundred gliders, towed by their Halifax tug-planes, have left Tarrant Rushton this Sunday morning to join the armada of three hundred Allied craft that are to land behind enemy lines in the Netherlands. Operation Market Garden is in the air and the Tarrant Rushton planes are towing the British 1st Airborne Division towards the farthest dropping zone, around Oosterbeek, four miles west of the great bridge over the Neder Rijn, the Lower Rhine at Arnhem.

Footnote This was the bridge too far. The Arnhem landings were a display of euphoric Allied over-confidence in the face of a mass of information that should have caused more than momentary reconsideration.
   Aerial photographs showed German tanks only a short distance from the drop-zone and Dutch resistance had reported "battered Panzer divisions" in Holland to refit. Furthermore there was an Enigma-coded intercept released two days before the operation was launched, stating that German Army Group B, under Field-Marshal Walther Model who was a veteran of the great tank battles in the Ukraine, had moved his headquarters to Oosterbeek; the Tafelberg Hotel to be precise, which lay between the drop-zone and the target – the Arnhem bridge over the Rhine. These were no ordinary enemy troops – they were the 2nd SS Panzer Corps, comprising the crack 9th and 10th SS Panzer Divisions.
   All this was known, but Montgomery – in the words of Lieutenant General Walter Bedell Smith, Chief of Staff at SHAEF [Supreme Headquarters Allied Expeditionary Force] – "simply waved my objections airily aside". Eisenhower, the Supreme Commander, admitted in 1966 that "I not only approved Market Garden, I insisted on it". He had on 5 September been so optimistic about the course of the war that he went as far as to declare "the defeat of the German armies is now complete". See the entry for 14 November, for their reaction.

22 September   **Ottawa conference VIPs fly into Poole.**

British VIPs returning from the Ottawa Conference have flown back into Poole Harbour aboard a BOAC Boeing Clipper.
   The party includes the Chief of the Imperial General Staff, Sir Alan Brooke, the First Sea Lord, Admiral Sir Andrew Cunningham, and the Chief of Air Staff, Sir Charles Portal.

Summer 1944. Lulworth Ranges. Captured German tank, being unloaded for British evaluation, with a backdrop of the Purbeck Hills. It is identified by Lieutenant-Colonel George Forty in his 'Bovington Tanks' (Dorset Publishing) as a Panzer Kpfe 111 Ausf J, mounting a 5-centimetre gun.

3 October 1944. Charlton Horethorne Naval Air Station, near Sherborne, showing a typical wartime grass aerodrome. The field lay to the north of Sigwell's Farm, and was an outstation of the Fleet Air Arm base at Yeovilton. The runways were mown which conveniently allowed the creation of more than would have been the case if they had been laid in concrete. The photograph was taken vertically, in the bright early morning of 3 October.

Examination of the print reveals a total of 72 aeroplanes – mostly squadrons of light trainers – dispersed around the edge of the field, with the probability of a few more concealed under the whiff of cloud and in hangars. There are 39 planes in the main parking area to the north-east of the airfield. The key explains the layout of the aerodrome. Blast bays and some of the smaller buildings survived until 1983, but the field itself was returned to agriculture after the war and is now under pasture and barley.

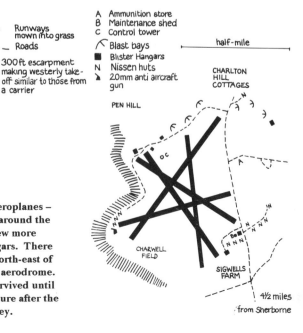

Key

Runways mown into grass
Roads
300 ft escarpment making westerly take-off similar to those from a carrier

A   Ammunition store
B   Maintenance shed
C   Control tower
⌒   Blast bays
■   Blister Hangars
N   Nissen huts
➤   2.0mm anti aircraft gun

half-mile

PEN HILL

CHARLTON HILL COTTAGES

CHARWELL FIELD

SIGWELLS FARM

4½ miles
from Sherborne

18 September 1944. Valkenswaard, The Netherlands. Fag-break beside a truck belonging to the 1st Battalion, the Dorsetshire Regiment, carrying the Wyvern badge of the 43rd (Wessex) Division on its nearside wing and a white '56' on a dull red square on the offside wing, showing its battalion number. The five-pointed star in the white circle is the universal marking for Allied vehicles in North-Western Europe.

13 May 1944. Kohima, central Burma. Only the chimney is still standing of the District Commissioner's bungalow, after the Japanese had been ousted from the ridge by the 2nd Battalion, the Dorsetshire Regiment. The tennis court (above it, to the right) was the scene of bitter hand-to-hand fighting at the climax of a three week battle in which the battalion lost 75 men.

29 September   **Dorsetmen enter the Reich.**

Infantrymen of the 1st Battalion of the Dorsetshire Regiment today formed the first infantry patrol to cross into Germany, though they are disappointed to have been forestalled by Sherman tanks of the Sherwood Rangers who have the distinction of being the first unit of the British Army to enter the Reich.

The Dorsets are operating in aid of the Guards Armoured Division in its breakout from the De Groote bridgehead. Trophies from the cross-border patrol include a German state flag and a black flag of the SS.

This evening, at the invitation of its supporting field battery, the CO of the Dorsets and his second in command fired token shells into Germany. One was painted with a message: "A present for Adolf Schickelgruber."

September   **Mudeford mine kills two sappers.**

Two members of a Royal Engineers mine-clearance team have been blown up whilst trying to remove a device from the beach at Avon Run Road, Mudeford, beside the entrance to Christchurch Harbour.

4 October   **Dorset troops see the V2s go up.**

The 1st Battalion of the Dorsetshire Regiment, holding what they call "The Island" at Bemmel, which is almost surrounded by Germans and linked only precariously with the main Allied advance, have seen several V2 rockets rise towards London from the enemy-occupied Hook of Holland.

They are being launched skywards from positions to the east, north-east and south-east. The rockets go straight up to a height of about ten kilometres before tilting into a 45 degree trajectory. The first to land on London hit Chiswick on 8 September and another fell the same evening at Epping.

Footnote None of the German vengeance weapons fell on Dorset, as the opposite coast had been captured before they became operational. The closest stray was a V1 flying-bomb that dropped on Boldre churchyard in the New Forest.

The Daily Telegraph saw the shape of things to come, if not thankfully to pass: "V2 indicates the kind of weapons with which the Third World War will be fought if there is one."

14 October   **Twelve drown in landing craft on Chesil Beach.**

An American tank landing craft, LCT A2454, was washed on to the Chesil Beach at Wyke Regis last night in mountainous seas. The state of the sea prevented the Weymouth lifeboat and a Portland dockyard tug from coming round the Bill to its aid.

Ten of the LCT's British crew were drowned despite the desperate efforts of the Fortuneswell Lifesaving Company who had run along the pebble bank from Portland and succeeded in firing a rocket-line into the stricken vessel. Two sailors were rescued by Coastguard Treadwell as a tremendous wave swept most of the crew and everything else that was moveable into the sea.

More lines were fired into the craft but as she shifted across the pebbles these fouled. Treadwell and Captain Pennington Legh were swept away, never to be seen again, as they struggled to free the lines. The four surviving rescuers also risked their lives to save two more of the sailors. Cyril Brown, wearing a lifebelt, struggled through the waves to get the line to the crewmen, and then had to be hauled ashore himself and taken to hospital. The line broke before the last crewman could be brought ashore and this time it was Albert Oldfield, without any safety line of his own, who managed to wade out to throw another line. The fourth man leapt from the boat and was pulled from the water.

Footnote The four surviving rescuers were awarded the Lloyd's silver medal for lifesaving but one, V.F. Stephens of Wyke Regis, died in a car crash before he could receive it at the reception in Weymouth Guildhall. Cyril Brown, of Portland, also received the Stanhope Medal, for the bravest deed of the year.

18 October   Hurn is RAF Hurn once again.

Formal control of Hurn Aerodrome was resumed by the Royal Air Force today on its transfer from the United States Army Air Force.

22 October   Celebrations as Fighter Command is revived.

There will be celebrations tonight at RAF Hurn and RAF Warmwell, along with every fighter aerodrome in the land, following the message to all units from Air Marshal Sir Roderick Hill, Commander-in-Chief Air Defence Great Britain. That title has been dropped and Fighter Command is being revived as the name for the air force allocated to defend Britain. Still under Sir Roderick Hill, it reverts to Air Ministry control. Officially, the change has been made because Air Defence Great Britain has now become chiefly offensive, but reasons of sentiment have influenced the decision, for the title was never popular with the pilots and ground crew of fighter squadrons.

Sir Roderick admits as much in his message: "To us, its heirs, Fighter Command is something more than a glorious name. I take this opportunity of paying my tribute to the illustrious past."

30 October   Poole bullets highlight a problem.

A Poole refuse disposal stoker had a close shave–a superficial face wound–when a cartridge clip exploded in his furnace. It has highlighted a serious danger and the public is asked to be more thoughtful with the disposal of explosives. Not that dustmen are going to lower their guard. Deadly objects are now lying around all over the country. Inevitably some of the smaller and less noticeable kinds will find their way into the dustbin.

October   **Coupon controller approves Christchurch cassocks.**

The vicar of Christchurch Priory, Canon W.H. Gay, writes in his monthly parish newsletter: "As some have questioned the legality of my appeal for clothing coupons to refit the choir with cassocks, may I state that the 143 coupons I have received will be sent to the Controller at Bournemouth, who will issue the needed permission to the tailor. I notice that most of the coupons have come from spinsters, widows and bachelors."

1 November   **RAF Hurn has closed.**

RAF Hurn has ceased to exist. At 00.00 hours today control passed from the Air Ministry to the Ministry of Civil Aviation and the military station became a civilian aerodrome.

1 November   **Poole craft attack Walcheren to free Antwerp.**

Twenty-five Poole landing craft manned by naval crews from the town's HMS Turtle base have landed commandos on Walcheren Island, the German-held strongpoint blocking the approaches to the Dutch port of Antwerp. Nine of the craft, the Support Squadron Eastern Flank, have been sunk and nine are immobilised.

Footnote The British commandos and Canadian ground forces took three days to capture the island. The channel to Antwerp was opened to Allied supply ships on 28 November.

11 November   **Dorsetmen are first gunners into Germany.**

The 94th Field Regiment of the Royal Artillery, mainly recruited from Bournemouth and Dorset in 1939, has become the first field gun force to cross the German frontier. It is supporting the Anglo-American offensive in the Geilenkirchen sector.

14 November   **4th Dorsets were heroes of Arnhem escapes.**

It became known today that it was largely owing to the matchless heroism of 250 men of the 4th Battalion of the Dorsetshire Regiment, part of the 43rd (Wessex) Division, that 2,400 out of the original 10,075 airborne troops succeeded in withdrawing from the Arnhem bridgehead on the night of 25 September.

　　Few, however, of the Dorsets escaped – and some of those had to swim the Neder Rijn to do so.

　　In the salient of the British advance, "The Island" at Bemmel, three Battalions of the Dorsetshire Regiment, the 1st, 4th and 5th, found themselves fighting in adjacent fields for the same "thumb print" on the map – the first time events had brought them together. Other Dorsets were able to give covering fire to men of the 4th Battalion as they rescued the survivors of the 1st Airborne Division and the Polish Parachute Brigade with a shuttle service of assault boats across the Neder Rijn [Lower Rhine].

By dawn on 26 September, at 06.00 hours, the intensity of enemy fire made further rescue crossings impossible.

3 December   The Home Guard stands down.

With the movement of the war into Europe throughout the second half of this year there have been the inevitable consequences on this side of the Channel and from today the Home Guard is stood down.

25 December 802 Piddlehinton Americans drown in the Channel.

The back-up troops for the clearance of the Germans from the Bretagne peninsula, the United States 262nd Infantry Division and part of the American 66th Infantry Division, left Piddlehinton Camp just before Christmas. They had arrived on 26 November and have now sailed for Cherbourg with their ultimate objective being to clear the enemy out of the U-boat pens at Brest.

There has, however, been an attack on the Allied convoy in the English Channel and one large transport vessel has been torpedoed, with considerable loss of life. The troopship *Leopoldville*, a Belgian passenger liner, was sunk yesterday by U-486 off Cherbourg, causing the deaths of 802 United States troops.

26 December   Blandford sees the cost of the Ardennes.

The news today is that General George Patton has at last been able to lead the tanks of the 3rd United States Army in the relief of Bastogne. The tide of the great German counter-offensive in the snowy forests of Luxembourg and southern Belgium, the Battle of the Ardennes, has been turned.

It has, however, been an achievement of American grit. The staunch determination of the American soldier since 16 December has prevented the Germans from coming back across the River Meuse.
Casualties are streaming into Dorset. Up to five hundred wounded Americans have been flown into Tarrant Rushton by the Dakotas in a single night, en route for the 22nd General Hospital at Blandford Camp.

Emergency supplies of penicillin have been requisitioned from British Drug Houses Limited. "Control of it is so tight," says director R.R Bennett, "that if I needed some for a dying brother I could not obtain it from my own firm but would have to apply through a government department."

Footnote The Ardennes reverses for the Germans were to be worse; estimated losses of 120,000 men with 600 tanks and assault guns, plus dozens of aircraft. There was nothing in reserve for another counter-attack.

29 December   **American freighter sinks in Worbarrow Bay.**

The *Black Hawk*, a United States steam-freighter, has sunk in Worbarrow Bay after being hit by a torpedo from a German U-boat.

December   **Posthumous VC for Dorchester's Arnhem hero.**

Captain Lionel Ernest Queripel of Dorchester has been posthumously awarded the Victoria Cross for his gallantry in the battle following the airborne landings at Arnhem. Born in 1920, he was fighting with the 10th Battalion, the Parachute Regiment.

The citation reads: "At Arnhem on 19 September 1944 Captain Queripel was acting as company commander of a composite company composed of men of three parachute battalions.

"At 14.00 hours on that day his company were advancing along a main road which runs on an embankment towards Arnhem. The advance was conducted under continuous machine-gun fire, which at one period became so heavy that the company became split up on either side of the road and suffered considerable loss. Captain Queripel at once proceeded to reorganise his forces, crossing and recrossing the road whilst doing so under extremely heavy and accurate fire. During this period he carried a wounded sergeant to the Regimental Aid Post under fire and was himself wounded in the face.

"Having reorganised his force, Captain Queripel personally led a party of men against a strong point holding up the advance. This strong point consisted of a captured British anti-tank gun, and two machine guns. Despite the extremely heavy fire directed at him, Captain Queripel succeeded in killing the crews of the machine guns and recapturing the anti-tank gun. As a result of this the advance was able to continue.

"Later in the same day Captain Queripel found himself cut off with a small party of men and took up a position in a ditch. By this time he had received further wounds in both arms. Regardless of his wounds and the very heavy mortar and Spandau fire, he continued to inspire his men to resist with hand grenades, pistols and the few remaining rifles. On at least one occasion he picked up and threw back at the enemy a stick grenade which had landed in the ditch.

"As, however, the enemy pressure increased, Captain Queripel decided that it was impossible to hold the position longer and ordered his men to withdraw. Despite their protests, he insisted on remaining behind to cover their withdrawal with his automatic pistol and a few remaining hand grenades. This is the last occasion on which he was seen.

"During the whole of a period of nine hours of confused and bitter fighting Captain Queripel displayed the highest standard of gallantry under most difficult and trying circumstances. His courage, leadership and devotion to duty were an inspiration to all."

December   **Shirburnian's posthumous VC for the bridge too far.**

Lieutenant John Grayburn, a platoon commander with the 2nd Battalion, the Parachute Regiment, has been posthumously gazetted with the Victoria Cross, for three days of gallant fighting on 17-20 September 1944. He went to Sherborne School.

His orders upon landing close to the bridge over the Rhine at Arnhem were to seize it and hold it.

After the north end of the bridge over the Rhine at Arnhem had been captured, Grayburn was ordered to take his platoon and seize and hold the southern end. This they kept attempting to carry out until casualties made further attempts futile: "He directed the withdrawal from the bridge personally and was himself the last man to come off the embankment into comparative cover.'"

Then, the citation continues, he occupied a house that stood in an almost indefensible position and managed to hold off sustained attack by infantry, mortars, tanks and self-propelled guns: "He constantly exposed himself to the enemy's fire while moving among and encouraging his platoon and seemed completely oblivious to danger."

Fire finally drove them from the building, on 19 September, and then John Grayburn led a fighting patrol back to the bridge to prevent the Germans from laying demolition charges. Despite being wounded in the back he continued to defend an untenable position.

In full view of a German tank he personally directed his men back to safety but stayed on the front-line, wounded and hungry and without having slept for days, and was killed on the night of 20 September.

The citation concludes: "There is no doubt that, had it not been for this officer's inspiring bravery, the Arnhem bridge could never have been held for this time."

December   **Henstridge airmen fight the Japs.**

Two Seafire squadrons from Henstridge Royal Naval Air Station, HMS *Dipper*, on the Somerset border at Stalbridge, are flying from the aircraft carrier HMS *Indefatigable* in offensive operations against the Japanese forces in the Pacific theatre.

887 and 894 (Fleet Air Arm) Squadrons comprise No.24 Royal Navy Fighter Wing. The Seafire is the marine version of the Spitfire.

Footnote On 1 April 1945, HMS *Indefagitable* became the first British carrier to be hit by a Japanese kamikaze plane. Among the pilots of 887 Squadron was Sub-Lieutenant R. Lygo, who would retire as Admiral Sir Raymond Lygo.

1939–1945. Opposite. 'Black-out' regulations and practicalities would go into history as an enduring memory of the Second World War.

BLACK-OUT

Motto : "KEEP IT DARK"

All external lights are totally extinguished. A small street-light ("star light") has been approved. Every occupier of buildings, factories, houses, flats, and rooms is responsible for darkening his own lights during the hours of "black-out."

1. **Lights in halls** and staircases of flats and tenements are responsibility of landlord.

2. **Illuminated advertisements** and signs are prohibited.

3. **Road vehicles.**—Cycle lamps must have top half of lamp glass obscured. Reflector or inside of semi-circular mask painted matt white or lined with white paper. Motor headlamps allowed only if screened and dimmed with officially approved mask. Side and rear lights of motor cars must have 1 in. aperture only, have paper dimming and be visible at 30 yards but invisible at 60 yards. Interior lights in buses, trams, etc., are screened and dimmed and switched off during alerts.

4. **Blinds and curtains.**—Opacity essential. Thick dark-coloured material, dark blue, or black, or dark green, glazed Holland, Lancaster or Italian cloth, rubberised cloth, or black or thick dark brown paper on battens.

5. **Testing material.**—The material should have passed the approved test of the British Standards Institution as sanctioned by the Ministry of Home Security, as set out in BS/ARP 23, 1939.

6. **Treating non-opaque blinds.**—Oil-bound water paint or distemper of dark colour. Apply with brush.

Formula : 1 lb. concentrated size. 3 lb. lamp black. $\frac{1}{2}$ gill gold size. Thoroughly mix size and lamp black and $2\frac{1}{2}$ gall. boiling water added. This sufficient for 80 sq. yards of material.

7. **Blinds not wholly light-tight fit.**—Paint round edges of windows with black paint.

8. **Hand Torches.**—Use permitted if shone downwards towards pavement. White light only allowed. Aperture of not more than 1 in. in diameter, and light dimmed by two pieces of tissue or equivalent paper.

9. **Penalties.**—There are heavy penalties for neglect to obey regulations. Police officers and members of Forces are entitled to enter premises to enforce the law. Wardens may only report infringements.

1944 hero. Killed at Arnhem.
Captain Lionel Queripel VC, of the 10th
Battalion, the Parachute Regiment came
from Dorchester.

After 17 September 1944. Arnhem. In defeat, defiance – as this picture in the Bundesarchiv proves. One third of the gliders of the British 1st Airborne Division that landed around Arnhem had flown from Tarrant Rushton in Dorset. There were a further 1,900 smaller aircraft involved in Operation Market Garden, with parachutists from the C-47 Dakotas bringing the number dropped at Arnhem to 8,000, and 10,075 as the total for the drop-zones as a whole. Of these, a significant proportion of the 2,490 who escaped back to Allied lines would be saved through the 'matchless heroism' of the 4th Battalion of the Dorsetshire Regiment, part of the 43rd (Wessex) Division.

1944 hero. Killed at Arnhem.
Lieutenant John Grayburn VC, of the 2nd
Battalion, the Parachute Regiment, went to
Sherborne School.

December 1944. Bournemouth. The author's parents, Gladys and Ted Legg at 21 Easter Road, Moordown, Bournemouth, received their last Christmas card of the present hostilities from Ted's brother, Arthur Legg who was having a good war as a despatch rider in Italy. It gave him a bike and absolute freedom; he always boasted that as far as taxation was concerned he never returned from the Western Desert. Of the Yanks, his lasting memory was the sheer scale and excesses of everything they did – always bringing enough spares to rebuild every piece of equipment half a dozen times. Arthur had more of a sense of humour than the rest of the family put together, myself included. He was in his second childhood and had written: 'The welding went on my silencer at Taranto the other day and now she sounds just like the good old grass track days, and by the way I can't get my licence taken away out here or in Cairo yet. You want to see the speed and noise we make, especially when on an Immediate Message. I had done 16,000 miles since coming to Italy in January [he wrote this on 14 June 1944, as 'typewriter and radio are tapping away'] and if old Deacon, Roe or Bryon [stuffy Bournemouth neighbours] was anywhere around in the busy streets of Bori or when I was in Cairo, their hair would stand on end and I guess I can't get the sack from the job till the Ruddy War is over. One-way streets mean nothing to us Drs [despatch riders] and the 'Red Caps' [military police] just don't know we are on SDR [Special Despatch Riding].' Arthur Legg lies in Talbot Village churchyard. If there is a life after death they will be enjoying something other than peace.

1945

Dakota C-47:
flying American Ardennes casualties
into Tarrant Rushton Aerodrome.

January   Warmwell joyrider takes a Spitfire to Cheselbourne.

Victor Swatridge of Dorchester Police wrote to me in 1971 with an account of an incident on a cold January night, apparently in 1945, when he was called by telephone at 2.45 am by the constable on the Broadmayne beat and told that a Spitfire had been stolen at 02.00 hours from Warmwell Aerodrome.

As there was a blizzard he thought this a little unlikely but the Observer Corps at Poundbury Camp confirmed they had heard a plane overhead at about 2.30 am. The missing plane had been said to have flown west and Poundbury reported the unmistakable sound of a Rolls-Royce Merlin engine. They reported it disappearing about six or seven miles to the north-east.

Moonlight followed the snow and Swatridge went with another officer on to the Dorset Downs around Cheselbourne in the centre of the county:

"At about 5 am on approaching Cheselbourne Water, to our amazement we saw a lighted hurricane lamp in the drive to a cottage. Naked lights were regarded as somewhat treasonable and very much frowned upon, as blackout regulations were strictly enforceable. Even the headlamps of cars were only allowed narrow slotted beams."

"I immediately nvestigated the reason for this breach and a woman, on answering my call at the cottage, stated that she had heard a plane overhead about two hours previously which appeared to have landed nearby. She went on to say, that she had been expecting her husband home on leave from France and it was the sort of stupid thing he would do, come by any means possible. She had placed the lighted lamp as a guide to him. Amazing as it seemed, we trudged on and clambered on to a high bank overlooking an unploughed cornfield where to our utter surprise we came upon tyre marks. On following them we found the missing fighter plane with its nose embedded in the hedge and bank at the other end of the field, on Eastfield Farm a quarter of a mile north-east of Cheselbourne church."

"Climbing onto the wing we found the cockpit lights burning but the 'bird' had flown. There was no trace of blood inside and we found footmarks in the snow made by the culprit, when walking way from the scene, but they quickly became extinct owing to the drifting snow. To cut a long story short I returned to the divisional station, after leaving a constable to guard the plane and a search party was sent out in daylight and a Canadian airman of the ground staff was arrested, having celebrated too liberally the previous night and in a rash moment embarked on this venturesome journey. There was only slight damage to the aircraft; the man was concussed and later dealt with by the authorities. So the escapade resolved itself."

6 February   **Cargo ship sunk off Dorset.**

Claimed by German submarine U-1017, a cargo ship that was torpedoed today off the Dorset coast has been identified as the *Everleigh*.   This 5,222-ton vessel was steaming down Channel, having left for New York.

20 February   **Christchurch hears of record 4,000-feet Bailey Bridge.**

The Experiment Bridging Establishment of the Royal Engineers, based beside the River Stour at Barrack Road, Christchurch, has heard that the longest of their Bailey Bridges yet constructed is now open for traffic across the River Meuse at Gennep, Netherlands.
    Its total span is more than 4,000 feet.
    Designed by Donald Coleman Bailey in 1939, the first prototype prefabricated steel bridge was put across the Stour at Christchurch, spanning seventy feet, on 1 May 1941. That took thirty-six minutes, from commencement to the first lorry reaching the other side.
    The new record-breaking bridge across the Meuse has taken ten days to erect, being delayed by the fact that its approaches were under two feet of water, and complicated by the height and speed of the river.
    It will enable 21 Army Group to intensify its relentless pressure against German forces behind the breached Siegfried Line, in the second phase of the Battle of the Rhineland. The defenders of Goch, at the confluence of the River Niers with the Meuse, surrendered yesterday to the Canadian 15th and 51st Divisions.
    South of Gennep, progress of the 52nd Division has been held up at Afferden by the floods.

25 February   **2nd Dorsets cross the Irrawaddy.**

The 2nd Battalion of the Dorsetshire Regiment today saw the "flyin' fishes play" as they crossed the Irrawaddy. Now, in Kipling's words, the British Army is "On the road to Mandalay." This has influenced the Dorsets' current battle cry, parodying *The Green Eye of the Yellow God* by J. Milton Hayes: "There's a dirty white pagoda to the east of Payadu."

12 March   **Burton Bradstock pensioners save crashed pilot.**

A Martinet from the Armament Practice Camp at Warmwell Aerodrome today developed engine problems over the Chesil Beach bombing range. The pilot crash-landed at Burton Mere, on the coast between Swyre and Burton Bradstock, but found himself trapped in the wreckage.
    Two heroes ignored the flames which were about to engulf the aircraft and untangled the pilot's feet. They were Miss Harriette Evelyn Bendy, aged 68, and Levi Rogers, aged 65, from Burton Bradstock. As they pulled the shocked airman to safety his aeroplane became an inferno.

19 March Christchurch Aerodrome goes to Transport Command.

RAF Christchurch was today transferred from No.11 Group, Fighter Command, to 46 Group, Transport Command. It is to be a satellite airfield to the major transport base on the western side of the New Forest at Ibsley, between Ringwood and Fordingbridge.

In the past nine months, Christchurch Aerodrome has been used as a diversionary airfield when intended destinations were closed by fog or other bad weather. Incoming flights from across the Channel have brought Allied wounded and German prisoners.

Aircraft types visiting Christchurch have included the Boston, Liberator, Stirling, and Douglas C-47 Dakota.

20 March   2nd Dorsets help take Mandalay.

Having left twenty-seven dead along the road to Mandalay, the 2nd Battalion of the Dorsetshire Regiment have arrived and are mopping up opposition as the Japanese withdraw.

General Sir Oliver Leese, Commander-in-Chief Allied Land Forces South-East Asia, visited the men this afternoon and told them they would have to make the next four hundred miles to Rangoon before the monsoon broke–though this time, he promised, they would not have to walk all the way.

Hearing the news of the capture of the ancient Burmese capital, Winston Churchill remarked: "Thank God they've at last got to a place I can pronounce!"

21 March   6th Airborne Division leaves Tarrant Rushton.

The British 6th Airborne Division, with its sixty Halifax tug-planes and their Hamilcar and Horsa gliders, is today leaving Tarrant Rushton Aerodrome for its new location, RAF Woodbridge.

This Suffolk airfield is closer to the division's next objectives, on the far side of the Rhine.

Footnote These landings, Operation Varsity, began at 09.54 hours on 24 March and continued for three hours; 6th Airborne took Hamminkein and the bridges over the River Issel. Fifty-two of the ex-Tarrant Rushton gliders landed successfully.

March   Duchess of Kent visits Blandford.

HRH the Duchess of Kent has visited the 22nd General Hospital of the United States Army, which now works with the 125th, 131st and 140th General Hospitals in a major medical complex across the former Anson-Craddock Lines at Blandford Camp.

It has received 17,000 patients of the long-term type, many of whom are needing complicated surgery. The commander is Lieutenant-Colonel Leonard D. Heaton.

March   **Poles sink U-boat in Poole Bay.**

Polish pilots have claimed a U-boat in the Channel, sunk in the south-east extremity of Poole Bay, towards the Isle of Wight.

9 April   **Warmwell ceases to be an operational airfield.**

152 Squadron, who have been operating at Warmwell since the dark days of 1940, have been withdrawn and the station is now retained only for training, by the Central Gunnery School.

17 April   **Puddletown lad dies forcing the Argenta Gap.**

Trooper James Legg, aged 21, from Puddletown, serving with the Queen's Bays, has been killed in action in Italy. He drove the first tank to force its way through the enemy's main defensive line in the Argenta Gap.

26 April   **BOAC Lancastrian flies from Hurn to Sydney.**

The first Lancastrian of British Overseas Airways Corporation's new fleet has landed in Australia at the end of a proving flight that lasted fifty-three hours. The airliner, G-AGLF carried the markings of the RAF's South-East Asia theatre but was on a pathfinding flight to determine the feasibility of a peacetime service.
    After flying out of Britain from RAF Hurn on 23 April the airliner touched down en route at Lydda in Palestine, Karachi in India, Ratmalana in Ceylon, and Learmonth in Western Australia.
    The pre-war flying-boat service from Southampton Water used to take nine days, but though so much faster, the Lancastrian has room for bunks and seats for only six passengers.
    The Empire flying-boat used to carry twenty-four passengers.

4 May   **Dorsets hear there is no longer a war in northern Europe.**

Cipher clerks to the units of the Dorsetshire Regiment in Germany received the signal at 20.50 hours today – "all offensive ops will cease from receipt of this signal."
    In other words, it's over.
    "Orders will be given to all troops to cease fire 08.00 hours tomorrow Saturday 5 May. Full terms of local German surrender arranged today for 21 Army Group front follow."
    The times are stated in British Double Summer Time and the Instrument of Surrender was signed by General-Admiral von Friedeburg, the emissary of Grand Admiral Karl Doenitz who is exercising command in Schleswig-Holstein in place of Hitler, and General Kinzel, Field-Marshal Ernst von Busch's Chief of Staff.
    It unconditionally surrenders all enemy forces in northern Germany and was signed at 18.30 hours in the Tactical Headquarters of Field-Marshal Sir Bernard Montgomery on Lüneburg Heath.

8 May **VE Day.**

15.00 hours. The war in Europe is officially at an end. Street parties, bonfires and church services will mark VE Day this Thursday evening.

9 May **Dorset gunners to occupy the Channel Islands.**

The officers commanding the German garrison on the Channel Islands today surrendered aboard the destroyer HMS *Bulldog*. The islands, which in normal times have their main English port at Weymouth, were passed by during the Battle of Normandy to avoid unnecessary Allied and civilian casualties.

The War Office contingency plan, prepared for the present eventuality, is for the Channel Islands to be occupied, garrisoned and then demilitarised by the 522nd (Dorset) Coast Regiment of the Royal Artillery.

This unit will cease to exist as such and be reformed for the purpose, as the 618th (Dorset) Garrison Regiment, Royal Artillery.

10 May **U-boats surface and surrender at Portland.**

U-249 surfaced in the English Channel at 09.22 hours yesterday and Oberleutnant Kock sent a signal to the Royal Navy that he wished to surrender.

The frigates HMS *Amethyst* and *Magpie* escorted the U-boat into Weymouth Bay this morning. She was the first German submarine to surrender, anywhere in Europe, and this afternoon U-825 followed her into Portland Harbour.

It is also understood that U-1023 has come into Weymouth as the surrender of Grand Admiral Karl Doenitz's fleet gathers pace.

12 May **Dorsets in first victory parade.**

The 5th Battalion of the Dorsetshire Regiment marched past Lieutenant-General Brian Horrocks, the commander of the 30th Corps, at Bremerhaven today in the first victory parade to be held in Germany.

16 May **Isle of Wight villagers send their prize to Portland.**

Villagers at Freshwater on the Isle of Wight were amazed when a U-boat surfaced offshore and requested someone to take its surrender. Freshwater has a parish councillor or two but it has no mayor or any one of the kind of standing that a German naval officer might respect. Anyway it has no port facilities apart from a beach and the inhabitants considered they were in line for a rollicking from the Royal Navy.

So U-776 was asked to surrender somewhere else and it departed for Portland Harbour. Someone in the Isle of Wight has turned up a splendid opportunity. Think of how he might have answered that inevitable question: "Granddad, what did you do in the war?"

FROM : EXFOR MAIN :	DATE-TOO 04 2050 B

TO : FOR ACTION : FIRST CDN ARMY : SECOND BRIT ARMY :

L of C : GHQ AA TPS : 79 ARMD DIV :

EXFOR REAR : ´

FOR INFM : SECOND TAF : EXFOR TAC : 22 LIAISON HQ :

GO 411 A SECRET . all offensive ops will cease from receipt this signal .
orders will be given to all tps to cease fire 0800 hrs tomorrow saturday
5 may . full terms of local German surrender arranged today for 21 ARMY GP
front follow . emphasise these provisions apply solely to 21 ARMY GP fronta
and are for the moment excl of DUNKIRK . ack

IN CIPHER if liable
to interoeption

DOP

EMERGENCY

R H Belchem

——————— BGS .

Copy to: All Branches Main HQ 21 Army Group
War Diary (2)

4 May 1945. Secret – the signal from Field-Marshal Montgomery's headquarters, telling all Allied units in north-west Europe that the German war was over, with 'all offensive ops' to 'crease from receipt of this signal' though excluding 'for the moment' the enemy enclave that had been left behind at Dunkirk.

18.30 hours, 4 May 1945. Field-Marshal Sir Bernard Montgomery (seated above, standing right) brings the European war to an end. In the next couple of hours the message will be with the troops in the field – that unless they are attacked there is to be no more fighting.

Instrument of Surrender

of

All German armed forces in HOLLAND, in

northwest Germany including all islands,

and in DENMARK.

1. The German Command agrees to the surrender of all German armed forces in HOLLAND, in northwest GERMANY including the FRISIAN ISLANDS and HELIGOLAND and all other islands, in SCHLESWIG-HOLSTEIN, and in DENMARK, to the C.-in-C. 21 Army Group. This to include all naval ships in these areas. These forces to lay down their arms and to surrender unconditionally.

2. All hostilities on land, on sea, or in the air by German forces in the above areas to cease at 0800 hrs. British Double Summer Time on Saturday 5 May 1945.

3. The German command to carry out at once, and without argument or comment, all further orders that will be issued by the Allied Powers on any subject.

4. Disobedience of orders, or failure to comply with them, will be regarded as a breach of these surrender terms and will be dealt with by the Allied Powers in accordance with the accepted laws and usages of war.

5. This instrument of surrender is independent of, without prejudice to, and will be superseded by any general instrument of surrender imposed by or on behalf of the Allied Powers and applicable to Germany and the German armed forces as a whole.

6. This instrument of surrender is written in English and in German.

   The English version is the authentic text.

7. The decision of the Allied Powers will be final if any doubt or dispute arises as to the meaning or interpretation of the surrender terms.

B. L. Montgomery
Field-Marshal

4 May 1945
1830 hrs

10 May 1945. Weymouth. U-249 is the first German U-boat to surrender. She had signalled her intention to the Royal Navy and this rendezvous was arranged in Weymouth Bay, prior to her being led into Portland Harbour.

1945. Badge of the Dorsetshire Regiment, now being worn from Burma to the Baltic.

30 May 1945. Blandford Camp. American colour party at the opening of Roosevelt Park.

30 May 1945. Blandford Camp. Memorial day for the men of the 22nd General Hospital of the United States Army. They remember the dead of World War Two and the passing of President Franklin D. Roosevelt who died last month, on 12 April.

30 May   **Roosevelt Park opened at Blandford.**

The first overseas memorial to the late President of the United States, Roosevelt Park inside the confines of Blandford Camp, was declared open today will an address by Colonel Daniel J. Fourrier of the US Army. A colour party fired ceremonial rounds.

The park is dedicated "to the everlasting memory of our fellow soldiers, at home and abroad, who gave their lives in this war, so that we who live may share in the future a free and better world".

It has been provided through voluntary contributions of members of the Army Medical Department with the landscaping being designed by a patient, Private George H. Stuber. Colonel Fourrier handed the park over to Colonel C. Topham of the Royal Engineers who received it on behalf of the British Army.

A six-foot high monument is under construction to enshrine the ideals behind the park permanently in stone.

June   **Gunnery School leaves and Warmwell closes.**

The RAF aerodrome at Warmwell closes this month with the departure of the Central Gunnery School for Sutton Bridge, Lincolnshire.

June   **Sherborne School's 242 death toll.**

The roll of honour published in The Shirburnian school magazine, during the course of the war, has now accounted for two hundred and forty-two lives. It compares with a death toll of two hundred and eighteen in the Great War, but Sherborne School was then far smaller.

The most distinguished of the Old Boys in the present conflict was mathematician Alan Turing who broke the German 'Enigma' cipher codes, and the bravest Lieutenant J.H. Grayburn, of Abbey House, who was posthumously awarded the Victoria Cross for his conspicuous gallantry on the bridge at Arnhem. John's was among the first VCs to be won for the Parachute Regiment and the only one by a Shirburnian in this war.

15 July   **Flying Fortress crash-lands at Christchurch.**

American aircrew being brought to Bournemouth for a period of leave had a lucky escape today at Christchurch Aerodrome.

Flying Fortress 866, carrying men of the 306th Bombardment Group from Thurleigh, Bedfordshire, overshot the western boundary of the notoriously short airfield. It plunged into scrubland. The near-side port engine was ripped out but the aircraft then came to a halt without exploding. No one was hurt.

26 July   **It is Declaration Day.**

The Conservative Party smarted today as the results were announced, confirming that a landslide of votes in the General Election, held on 5

July, is set to oust war-leader Winston Churchill and put a Labour administration in his place. Pre-war memories are blamed for the scale of the socialist success which has surprised the world in its rejection of the country's saviour. It is regarded as an unwarranted dismissal.

Even in Dorset, which must be quite blue, it has been a close-run thing for the Conservatives to hold their seats. The East Dorset constituency returned Lieutenant-Colonel Mervyn Wheatley with 26,561 votes against 25,093 to his Labour opponent Lieutenant-Commander Cyril Fletcher-Cooke, with Liberal Colonel Mander having the remaining 8,975. Out of 80,816 on the registers there was a 60,629 poll, including 8,352 votes from men and women in the armed services.

Footnote Clement Attlee became Prime Minister on 27 July with Ernest Bevin as Foreign Secretary, Sir Stafford Cripps at the Board of Trade, and Hugh Dalton as Chancellor of the Exchequer.

15 August   Henstridge pilots celebrate VJ Day.

It is victory over Japan Day. Nowhere in Dorset has the celebration been more heart-felt than in Stalbridge and in particular the Wrens' Quarters on the Dorset side of HMS Dipper, the Royal Naval Air Station at Henstridge which literally straddles the county boundary with Somerset.

Here a bonfire has been kept burning all night, despite a soaking at 05. 00 hours when the rain intensified, having been started a few minutes after midnight when the station Tannoy had roused everyone from sleep: "Attention everybody. Attention. Japan has surrendered." The party began, and is still carrying on in the Swan at Stalbridge. This was still an operational air station. VE Day had been only half the story. For the young New Zealand pilots and others under training the war was still a going concern and their lives under risk in what was becoming the "forgotten war". The atomic bombs ended all that. Leaflets dropped on Hiroshima on August 4th warned: "Your city will be obliterated unless your Government surrenders."

That blow was delivered from a single United States Army Air Force Boeing B-29 Superfortress, *Enola Gay* piloted by Paul Tibbets Junior, on the 6th. The aircraft was named for the pilot's mother and its bomb was called 'Little Boy'. Then Nagasaki was threatened its "rain of ruin the like of which has never been seen on earth". That was wrought by the 'Fat Man' which was dropped from another B-29, *Bock's Car*, on the 9th.

The third atom bomb, standing-by and probably for Tokyo, did not have to be dispatched. Japan began the surrender process four days ago.

21 August   'Our man in Berlin' – Lindsay is dead.

Sir Ronald Lindsay, of Stepleton House near Blandford, died today. The retired diplomat was born in 1877. He rose through the ranks at the Foreign Office to become an under-secretary in 1920 and progressed to the highest postings in the service – being ambassador to Berlin [1926-28] and Washington [1930-39]. When he bowed out the war, as they say, was an extension of diplomacy by other means.

The classical Stepleton House and its park, where Peter Beckford wrote the classic book on fox-hunting, has passed to Sir Ronald's nephew, Lord Crawford.

22 August   US Ambassador unveils Portland's memorial.

Portland's memorial to the Americans of V Corps who passed through the harbour en route to D-Day and the fierce fighting on Omaha beach was unveiled today by the United States Ambassador, Gil Winant.

He was welcomed by the chairman of Portland Urban District Council, A. N. Tattersall, after driving along the newly re-named Victory Road.

The stone is in Victoria Gardens and the Stars and Stripes flies above beside the Union Jack. Disappointingly, it has been a very wet Wednesday.

Footnote "Fine, fine, perfectly fine," was Winant's famous remark of the war; which he kept repeating over the transatlantic telephone when Roosevelt told him of Pearl Harbor. By now, however, he was engulfed in personal problems and would shoot himself in 1947, after his return to the United States. He is said to have set his heart on Winston Churchill's daughter, but Sarah Churchill was unable to reciprocate his love.

31 August   Canford School counts 139 dead.

Canford School's roll of war dead has closed at a total of 139 lives, from this its first war. As the school was founded in 1923 it happened that all Old Canfordians were of an age to serve and indeed nearly a thousand of them held commissions.

August   Penicillin works wonders at Shaftesbury.

The apparently miraculous cures brought about at Shaftesbury Military Hospital, Guy's Marsh [now a Borstal] with M&B tablets have now been upstaged by the use of penicillin. This has reversed impossible infections which previously would have certainly killed even the strongest soldiers. It has taken years to bring the drug into commercial production; in 1942 the entire world supply was needed to treat a single case of meningitis.

Remarkable surgery is taking place too. Strabismus is being corrected by an easing of the muscles around the eyeball. Major John Charnley has carried out a hip-replacement operation at Shaftesbury which was as much a feat of carpentry as an exercise of the surgeon's craft.

August   British military back in Blandford Camp.

The British Army has returned to Blandford Camp – which saw out the war as a major American General Hospital – with the arrival of the 1st and 2nd Searchlight Regiments, Royal Artillery, in the huts of the Craddock and Benbow Lines. These units will train conscripts who have been called up to serve their national service with the Royal Artillery.

THE PILOT, 1940-1945   E.A.P.

To the
Right Honourable Winston S. Churchill, M.P.

No specious facile promise, no smooth word
Fell from your lips when the grim stage was set
For the stern test of war.   You offered then
Nothing but blood and tears and toil and sweat.

Brave words—that nerved the hand to grasp the sword,
And purchase Victory at the price of pain—
Wherein, great pilot of the Ship of State,
Did Britain find her very soul again !

E. A. Penny

1945-46. Tribute to Churchill, from the Dorset Year Book.

6 August 1945. Hiroshima's bomb—'brighter than the sun'—but another would be needed to bring about the surrender process.

August 1945. Yanks go home. Troopship 'Queen Elizabeth' prepares to sail down Southampton Water for the United States, with tugs at her bow and a flypast salute overhead.

22 August 1945. Portland. Depressing day in the rain for United States Ambassador Gil Winant, unveiling Portland's tribute to the Americans who fell on Omaha Beach. Winant's life was being destroyed for the love of Sarah Churchill.

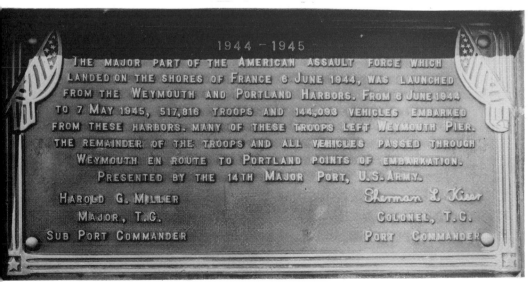

1944 – 1945
THE MAJOR PART OF THE AMERICAN ASSAULT FORCE WHICH LANDED ON THE SHORES OF FRANCE 6 JUNE 1944, WAS LAUNCHED FROM THE WEYMOUTH AND PORTLAND HARBORS. FROM 6 JUNE 1944 TO 7 MAY 1945, 517,816 TROOPS AND 144,093 VEHICLES EMBARKED FROM THESE HARBORS. MANY OF THESE TROOPS LEFT WEYMOUTH PIER. THE REMAINDER OF THE TROOPS AND ALL VEHICLES PASSED THROUGH WEYMOUTH EN ROUTE TO PORTLAND POINTS OF EMBARKATION. PRESENTED BY THE 14TH MAJOR PORT, U.S. ARMY.

HAROLD G. MILLER
MAJOR, T.C.
SUB PORT COMMANDER

Sherman L. Kiser
COLONEL, T.C.
PORT COMMANDER

18 September   **First Jap prisoners arrive home at Poole.**

The first BOAC flying-boat to bring repatriated prisoners-of-war home to Britain from Japan has touched down in Poole Harbour, amid sensational press interest in the men's stories of degrading and inhuman treatment.

They were given a civic welcome at a reception on Poole Quay. Many thousands are en route home by sea and air.

18 September   **Pan Am Skymaster drops into Hurn from New York.**

An ex-military C-54 Skymaster of Pan American Airways has landed at Hurn Aerodrome from La Guardia Airport, New York, in a proving flight that took seventeen hours. The airliner, carrying nine crew and ten staff as observers, stopped off en route at Gander in Newfoundland and Rineanna in Eire.

This was the first time a four-engined land-plane – as distinct from a flying-boat – has crossed the Atlantic on a civilian flight.

Former Halifax bombers, in conversions known as Haltons, are currently operating from Hurn on the BOAC route to Lagos and the other West African colonies.

19 September   **'Lord Haw-Haw' remembered at Farnham.**

The Fascist hireling and traitor William Joyce smiled in the dock at the Old Bailey today as the black-capped judge told him: "You will be hanged by the neck until you are dead." He gave a Nazi salute to people at the back of the court.

The voice of Radio Berlin, for its wartime broadcasts to England, he had been captured near the Danish frontier, by the British troops in the last week of May. He was identified and brought to London where he was charged with treason, on the grounds that although Irish-born he had put himself under His Majesty's protection by obtaining a United Kingdom passport.

"Lord Haw-Haw" is remembered in Dorset for his pre-war cottage sojourn at Farnham, near Blandford, as the guest of Captain George Pitt-Rivers.

3 October   **Christchurch colonel fires a V2.**

Colonel Raby, the Director of the Signals Research and Development Establishment at Christchurch Aerodrome and Steamer Point, Highcliffe, today test-fired a German V2 rocket which he had reconstructed from captured parts. It has been flown northwards, along the coast from Cuxhaven, near Bremerhaven, into the North Sea off Denmark.

This has been a secret test, codenamed Operation Backfire, and tomorrow another rocket will be fired. Raby's establishment is working on the first British guided weapons.

Footnote A third V2 was fired by the British team on 15 October 1945; this time the world's press would be invited and bill it as "the first Allied test-firing of a V2 rocket".

October   Blandford hospital staff leave on the 'Queen Mary'.

The 22nd General Hospital of the United States Army has finally pulled out of Blandford Camp.

The last of its staff are now sailing back across the Atlantic from Southampton aboard the liner *Queen Mary*.

25 November   Five Poole flying-boats exit for Argentina.

Argentina, a Sandringham 2 flying-boat which is a Mark V Sunderland powered by American Pratt and Whitney Twin Wasp engines and fitted out for forty-five passengers, lifted off from Poole Harbour today for Buenos Aires. She has been sold to Dodero, the Argentine airline, along with the similar Uruguay and three Sandringham-3 flying-boats.

These have more spacious accommodation for their twenty-one passengers and are intended for longer flights. They are the *Brazil*, *Inglaterra*, and *Paraguay*. Each is being delivered across the Atlantic by a BOAC crew with Argentineans aboard as observers. The flight time is estimated at thirty-six hours.

31 December   Home Guard disbanded.

Today has seen the last rites for the Home Guard as it is finally disbanded by the War Office.

"The spirit of comradeship and service which was brought to life by service to the Dorset Home Guard must never be allowed to die," says its last Commander, General Henry Jackson.

December   Japan's PoWs still in Hell at Shaftesbury.

The pitiful casualties of this war, beyond the help of surgery and drugs, are the psychologically distressed ex-prisoners of the Japanese who have been brought home from the Far East to recover at Shaftesbury Military Hospital [subsequently Guy's Marsh Borstal]. Many are also emaciated but it is the mental damage that will take longer to correct. They suffer horrific memories when they are awake and lapse into agonising nightmares in sleep.

Such dehumanised wrecks become even more pathetic as they regain their physical strength without a comparable recovery from mental anguish. They are men returned from Hell.

Their ordeal is worse in its way than the more clear-cut cases on life's edge with tuberculosis. These three wards would once have been one-way nursing towards death but here expectations and hope have been transformed as a result of the introduction of the wonderdrug streptomycin.

December   **Plaque at Portland commemorates the logistics.**

The 14th Major Port of the Transportation Corps of the United States Army has presented a bronze plaque to Portland dockyard commemorating the logistics of the invasion of Europe:

"1944-1945. The major part of the American assault force which landed on the shores of France 6 June 1944, was launched from the Weymouth and Portland Harbors. From 6 June 1944 to 7 May 1945, 517,816 troops and 144,093 vehicles embarked from these harbors. Many of these troops left Weymouth Pier. The remainder of the troops and all vehicles passed through Weymouth en route to Portland points of embarkation.

"Presented by the 14th Major Port, U.S.Army. Harold G. Miller, Major, T.C. [Transportation Corps] Sub Port Commander. Sherman L. Kiser, Colonel, T.C. Port Commander."

1945-46. Off Brownsea Island, Poole Harbour. Hythe-class Short Sunderland Mark-3 flying-boats, formerly RAF transports with gun turrets (above), though these are removed in the second picture (below). They carry Transport Command markings and operate with British Overseas Airways on the Empire route to India, Singapore and Australia. OQZS 'Hanbury' is seen on take-off (above), heading westwards up the Main Channel and destined for Bombay. The passenger launch (below) is speeding away from OQZC 'Hamilton' and OQZH 'Harwich'.

3 October 1945. Cuxhaven, British-occupied Germany. Opposite. Under the command of Colonel Raby, from the Signals Research and Development Establishment at Christchurch, Royal Engineers prepare to test-fire a captured German V2 rocket. It will land in the North Sea, off the Danish coast. Rocket expert John Pitfield identifies this as a rebuilt 'British' V2 from its dazzle-pattern paintwork which was used to make it visible in the sky.

February   War's upheavals bring Uplands School to Parkstone.

Uplands School, which was founded in 1903 at St Leonards-on-Sea, Sussex, is on the move to Parkstone. It has come via Monmouthshire, where it was evacuated when invasion threatened in 1940, and it had been hoped to return to Sussex in 1944 but the flying bombs caused these plans to be abandoned.

   Instead it is coming to Parkstone, to the buildings of a sister church school for girls, Sandecotes, which was itself closed in 1940 when the buildings were requisitioned by the military.

1 July   2nd Dorsets on Tokyo's 'Buck House' guard.

The 2nd Battalion of the Dorsetshire Regiment has been hastily consigned to Tokyo in Operation Primus, to relieve the New Zealanders on ceremonial guard duties in the Japanese capital. The Americans are its army of occupation on the streets. Dorset sentries are preparing for what they call "No 1, Buck House guard" – at the Imperial Palace.

   The rosters assume that the battalion's eight hundred men will be able to maintain two hundred sentries at posts around the city.

Footnote Sharing the imperial guard with the Americans was not quite on Buckingham Palace lines, Lieutenant-Colonel Geoffrey White recalled in *Straight on for Tokyo:* "It is not easy when your companion on the post allows himself rather a more relaxed form of stand-at-ease, and it is most disconcerting to have a doughnut offered you on the end of a bayonet."

1944–45. Supermarine Seafire, the naval version of the famous fighter, adapted for use on aircraft-carriers by Airspeed Limited at Christchurch.

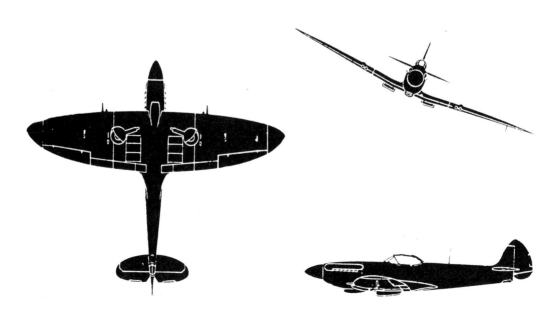

I·N·D·E·X

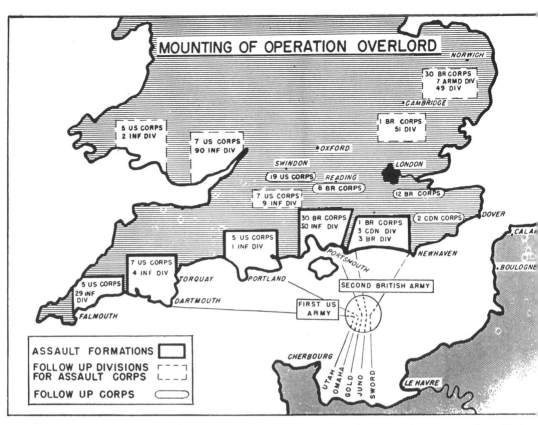

5–7 June 1944. Dorset's place on the assault map, as the springboard for the American First Infantry Division to attack Omaha Beach. Their comrades in the Second Infantry Division are the back-up troops, waiting in South Wales.

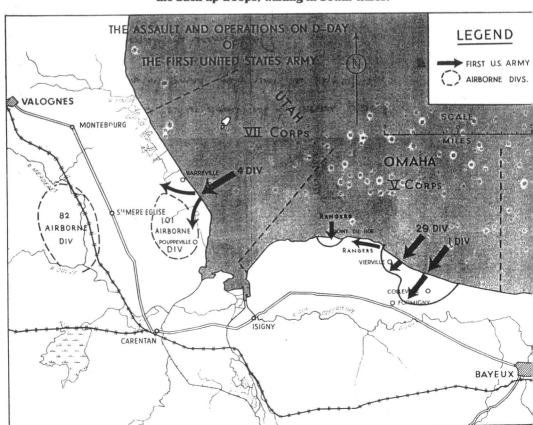